An Approach to Criticism

An Approach to Criticism

John Ginger

HODDER AND STOUGHTON
LONDON SYDNEY AUCKLAND TORONTO

ISBN 0 340 11784 2

First published 1970
Fifth impression 1977
Copyright © 1970 John Ginger

Printed offset litho and bound in Great Britain for
Hodder and Stoughton Educational,
a division of Hodder and Stoughton Limited,
Mill Road, Dunton Green, Sevenoaks, Kent,
by Cox & Wyman Ltd, London, Fakenham and Reading

Preface

Many of the passages for appreciation in this book have already been used in class both at sixth form and university level. It was the accumulation of teaching material, and a consideration of the number of hours spent in searching for it, which gave me the idea that other teachers might find it useful—especially when their literary appreciation classes, however prized, are only an item in a sometimes demanding curriculum.

The actual presentation of this material in book form has raised some problems. I found that I was reluctant to relinquish my classroom right to guide, and intervene in, a discussion; and I have kept it in the form of the questions attached to each passage. They are, quite frankly, *leading* questions, which either point directly to my own interpretation of the work in question, or draw attention to the crux upon which interpretation seems ultimately to depend. Some teachers and students may prefer to use the extracts and ignore these questions. To those who do make use of them, I must make a provisional apology lest any seem too dogmatic, and confess that, apart from their inverted commas, some of the 'quotations' have very little in common with the real thing. This device, which has allowed me to present under a neutral flag both my own views and those with which I would disagree, proved too useful to resist.

For the sake of convenience the book has been divided into two parts to consider poetry and prose respectively. This arrangement is not intended to imply a rigid distinction, and in fact some sections of the introduction to Part I (in particular the discussion of imagery, diction and tone) are also relevant to Part II.

I should like to express my gratitude to Dame Ivy Compton-Burnett, Mr Laurens van der Post and Mr E. M. Forster for allowing me to quote from *A Family and a Fortune*, *A Bar of Shadow* and *A Passage to India*; and to Professor Molly Mahood for suggesting the Conrad: van der Post and Dickens: Henry James pairings.

Contents

Preface

PART 1   THE CRITICISM OF POETRY

Introduction: Making the poem—The shape—Metaphors and   3
    symbols—The words—The voice

    PASSAGES FOR ANALYSIS

 1   W. H. Auden   *His Excellency*   42
 2   Rupert Brooke   *The Dead*: Wilfred Owen   *Futility*   44
 3   G. M. Hopkins   *Spring and Fall*   47
 4   Thom Gunn   *On the Move*:   49
     Philip Larkin   *Essential Beauty*
 5   John Keats   *Ode on a Grecian Urn*:   54
     D. H. Lawrence   *Cypresses*
 6   Alexander Pope   from *Eloisa to Abelard*:   61
     George Crabbe   from *Peter Grimes*
 7   George Herbert   *Affliction*:   65
     G. M. Hopkins   *Carrion Comfort*
 8   W. B. Yeats   *He Bids his Beloved be at Peace*:   70
     Robert Graves   *Sick Love*
 9   Alexander Pope   from *An Epistle to Dr Arbuthnot*:   73
     R. S. Thomas   *Cynddylan on a Tractor*
10   Robert Graves   *The Cool Web* and *The Bards*   77
11   William Wordsworth   from *The Prelude*:   80
     Robert Frost   *The Most of It*
12   George Herbert   *Life*:   Ella Wheeler Wilcox *Guerdon* 84
13   Sophocles   chorus from *Oedipus at Colonus*,   87
     translated by R. C. Trevelyan, Gilbert Murray,
     Robert Fitzgerald

14 Andres Marvell   *The Definition of Love*:   91
    George Barker   *Love Poem*
15 T. S. Eliot   from *Ash Wednesday*

                                                                 97

PART 2   THE CRITICISM OF PROSE

Introduction   109

PASSAGES FOR ANALYSIS

 1 Charles Dickens   *David Copperfield*:   132
    Laurie Lee   *Cider with Rosie*
 2 Thomas Love Peacock   *Headlong Hall*:   137
    James Thurber   *My Life and Hard Times*
 3 Jane Austen   *Emma*   142
 4 Samuel Butler   *The Way of all Flesh*:   148
    John Galsworthy   *The Man of Property*
 5 Joseph Conrad   *The End of the Tether*:   153
    Laurens van der Post   *A Bar of Shadow*
 6 Charles Dickens *Bleak House*:   157
    Henry James   *The Bostonians*
 7 Graham Greene   *The Power and the Glory*   162
 8 Thomas Hardy   *The Return of the Native*:   166
    D. H. Lawrence   *The White Peacock*
 9 George Eliot   *Middlemarch*:   171
    E. M. Forster   *A Passage to India*
10 Evelyn Waugh   *A Handful of Dust*   177
11 Ivy Compton-Burnett   *A Family and a Fortune*   181
12 Henry James   *The Spoils of Poynton*:   190
    George Eliot   *Middlemarch*
13 Herman Melville   *Moby Dick*:   195
    William Faulkner   *Sanctuary*
14 Samuel Richardson   *Pamela*:   199
    Mary Webb   *Precious Bane*:
    Joyce Cary   *Herself Surprised*
15 James Joyce   *A Portrait of the Artist as a Young Man*   204

Suggestions for Further Reading   211
Acknowledgments   212

In ev'ry Work regard the Writer's End,
Since none can compass more than they intend;
And if the Means be just, the Conduct true,
Applause, in spite of trivial Faults, is due.

ALEXANDER POPE, *An Essay in Criticism*

PART 1   The criticism of poetry

INTRODUCTION

MAKING THE POEM

In 1859, a New England recluse copied out the following lines and put them away in her desk:

Safe in their Alabaster Chambers—
Untouched by Morning
And untouched by Noon—
Sleep the meek members of the Resurrection—
Rafter of Satin,
And Roof of stone.

Light laughs the breeze
In her Castle above them—
Babbles the Bee in a stolid Ear,
Pipe the Sweet Birds in ignorant cadence—
Ah, what sagacity perished here!

Either at this time or on some occasion during the next two years, she showed a copy of them to her sister-in-law, Sue; and the outcome of Sue's criticism was a new second stanza. The revised poem was sent to Sue next door with a note:

Safe in their Alabaster Chambers,
Untouched by Morning—
And untouched by Noon—
Lie the meek members of the Resurrection—
Rafter of Satin—and Roof of Stone—

Grand go the years—in the Crescent—above them—
Worlds scoop their Arcs—

And firmaments—row—
Diadems—drop—and Doges—surrender—
Soundless as dots—on a disc of Snow—

Perhaps this verse would please you better—Sue—Emily—

Sue replied with further criticism: 'I am not suited dear Emily
with the second verse—It is remarkable as the chain lightning
that blinds us hot nights in the Southern sky but it does not go with
the ghostly shimmer of the first verse as well as the other one—it
just occurs to me that the first verse is complete in itself and needs no
other, and can't be coupled—Strange things always go alone—as
that verse, and I guess you[r] kingdom doesn't hold one—I always
go to the fire and get warm after thinking of it, but I never can
again— . . . . Sue

Emily Dickinson turned to the problem of the second stanza
again, and produced the following versions:

Springs—shake the sills—
But—the Echoes—stiffen—
Hoar is the window—
And numb the door—
Tribes—of Eclipse—in Tents—of Marble—
Staples—of Ages—have buckled—there—

Springs—shake the Seals—
But the silence—stiffens—
Frosts unhook—in the Northern Zones—
Icicles—crawl from Polar Caverns—
Midnight in Marble—Refutes—the Suns—

She copied out the first of these and sent it round to Sue with a
further note which began 'Is this frostier?'. There is no record of the
sister-in-law's reply.

Evidently the poem continued to worry its author. It is probable
that, when she began to work on it again in 1861, she had already
been invited to contribute to the Springfield Daily Republican—hence the
revisions. But the lines that appeared in the newspaper on Saturday,
1 March 1862, under the heading 'The Sleeping' were those she had

written in 1859. A month later, she sent some poems to a literary acquaintance, T.W. Higginson. Amongst them were the two stanzas, 'Safe in their Alabaster Chambers' and 'Grand go the years' (the second taking the place of the published 'Light laughs the breeze').

Here is a good example of the debt owed to editorial research.[1] It is also an opportunity to watch the poet in the act of creating a poem. Why did the second stanza cause so much difficulty? Was Emily Dickinson too ready to accept her sister-in-law's judgment?—Or was Sue right, and had Emily recognized a valid criticism in the note brought round from next door?

The stanzas published in the *Springfield Daily Republican* were dated 'Pelham Hill, June 1861'. Emily Dickinson was fond of this place and had probably visited the old graveyard there. Even without biographical conjecture of this kind, we learn from her other poems that, like John Donne, she devoted a great deal of thought to death in both its physical and metaphysical aspects. This poem, like many of her others, is an attempt to communicate her own imaginative experience of it.

The poet is aware of two very different strands of feeling within herself. She is a Christian, and her religion teaches her to regard death as a sleep. She is also a person whose senses are alert in a more than usual degree; and reason tells her that death marks the end of sensory experience.

Sue had suggested a solution to the problem of the second stanza. Did the poem *need* a second? Wasn't the first stanza complete in itself?—But the poet's attempt to find a satisfactory second suggests that, fairly early in the poetic process, she had decided that the form her feelings were looking for was a two-stanza poem. The first stanza examines the 'sleep' idea, reveals it as a euphemism; the end of the stanza, when euphemism is abandoned, is the pivot on which the whole poem turns. The second stanza conveys the sense of deprivation.

The members of the resurrection sleep; they are at peace—*safe*. Here is the Christian comfort. But already another note has sounded. There is a troubling ambiguity about the first three lines. *Alabaster* may give us a picture of a palace ('marble halls')—though we remember that

---

[1] The different versions of this poem and the biographical material are given in *The Poems of Emily Dickinson*, edited by Thomas H. Johnson (Harvard University Press, 1955).

tombs were once made of alabaster. *Chambers* at first suggests rooms, perhaps the magnificent apartments of a palace. We are undecided: is this poem about the living or the buried dead? *Safe*, that dominant first chord, has suggested the former interpretation and encouraged us to suppress the cold and funereal associations of *alabaster*; it will also prompt the reading 'unharmed' for *untouched*. But at this stage the reason begins to rebel. To be 'touched' by morning and noon is to be warmed by the sun; to be 'untouched' is to remain cold, to be deprived. We look again at *alabaster*.

As we begin to see the direction the poet is taking, we become a little more cautious of *members of the resurrection*. The phrase, familiar in a Christian context, couples the two ideas of dying and immortality. But there are no further allusions in the poem to eternal life. Does the phrase, then, introduce an unexamined concept—a second-hand idea glibly parroted?—Or is this an intentional use of cliché? The second interpretation is more in keeping with the suspicion which the use of traditional euphemisms has already aroused.

Now, having shown us that she is playing with attitudes which are really foreign to her own experience, she confronts us with the truth. *Rafter of Satin*, which strangely contradicts our sensory experience (rafters hard, satin soft), plays on the same nerve as *alabaster* and *untouched*. *Rafters* belong, perhaps, with *safe* and *chambers*; but why of satin?—Until we jump the gap between the euphemistically employed 'members of the resurrection' (the dead) and the actual coffin, which has a padded lid and lies under a stone slab (*roof of stone*).

Here, second-hand ideas of death are relinquished; and we come to the poet's imaginative experience of it. When the body ceases to function, the life of the senses comes to an end. The sense of touch has already been mentioned. The sleepers were *untouched* by the sun. In the second stanza, man's total sensory experience is represented, metaphorically, by the sense of hearing. In the tomb, he can no longer hear the sounds of bees and birds and of the wind in the field above him. And the metaphors point the irony that it is now the 'inanimate' things that possess a kind of life: the breeze laughs from her stronghold (*castle*) in the living world (we are reminded here of the ambiguous palace-tomb of the first line); it is the wind now, which is *safe*—unchanging, unaffected by the extinction of the sensing creature. And the things of sense have become especially desirable. We listen. The bee *babbles*; the *sweet* birds *pipe*. With a grimly humorous return to the euphemisms of the first stanza, the unhearing dead are described, not as being deaf to these lovely sounds, but as *stolid*. They are insensitive, obtuse.

The half-mocking, half-regretful *Ah* heralds the concluding irony. The dead for all their former knowingness are now less fortunate than the birds singing over their graves. The hope which seemed to be offered in the borrowed phrase *members of the resurrection* has, within the context of this experience, been rejected. Latinisms—*cadence* and *sagacity*—with their stately suggestion of a funeral sermon—are a sombre foil to the joys of sense conveyed in simpler words, *babbles*, *pipe* and *sweet*.

Sue responded, as we have already seen, to the *coldness* of the first stanza. She had to 'go to the fire and get warm after thinking about it'. There is nothing cold about the second, and even though we may respond to the irony of the contrast, there is a danger that, in experiencing the essentially gay, light-hearted scene around the graveyard, we may lose sight of its inhabitants. Emily Dickinson accepted her sister-in-law's criticism. Instead of 'Light laughs the breeze', she needed a stanza which would convey the idea of the rift between the world of sense and the world of the dead without spoiling the cold effect of the picture created in the first. The idea of Nature which endures and continues, insensible to the passing of the individual, is essential to the poem; but in her first revision she turns away from Nature in its more immediate aspects and introduces it at a more awe-inspiring level: the stars in their courses. It is no longer gentle breezes and sweetly singing birds that ignore the sleepers, but planets that *scoop their arcs* and *row* through the *firmament* (like boats across a lake). The movement of the planets means the passing of time; and it is an easy jump to the synecdoche, *Diadems drop and Doges surrender*. The Dead are now the Great, the Rulers, whose disappearance is unmarked by the mighty rolling of the universe.

One image is salvaged from the former version. The Sleepers were deaf. Now it is the universe which is deaf. The passing of the Great is

Soundless as dots on a disc of snow

—a return to nature at a more intimate level, but in a quite different way from the idyllic scene sketched in the first version.

We have seen Sue's reaction to this revision, and we can infer

Emily Dickinson's inability to decide between the two from the fact that in March 1861 she allowed her first version to be published, and in April sent the second to Higginson. Was her critic right? And does the poet's own indecision reflect a half-formed dissatisfaction with both stanzas?

The imagery of 2b ('Grand go the years') is on the right scale and avoids the obtrusive prettiness of 2a. But 2b is very uneven. *Grand* for instance, is unfortunate; it evokes a military parade rather than the wheeling of universes. The rowing image is irrelevant and inaccurate; for, though interplanetary space may be thought of as a lake, *row* gives a quite unhelpful picture of the planet (and the inversion in this third line makes the image obscure). *Diadem* is an anticlimax after the universe imagery, and the allusion to the fall of the Venetian Republic limits us even more drastically and irrelevantly. The heavy alliteration of this line is purposeless; we may have an uneasy idea that it alone has dictated the choice of *Doges*. Significantly, it is the echo of 2a which arrests our attention. When we examine it, we find that it is also a development of an idea in the first stanza: the dead are *cold* in their chambers of alabaster, sealed off from the warm morning and noon sun. The simile *as dots on a disc of snow* is accurate and, with its reminder of intense cold, appropriate. It captures perfectly the idea of deprivation that the poet has wanted to communicate. And it does more. Our imagination is liberated by this picture of cold and silence, of the grave itself, perhaps, being inevitably but gently obliterated, of the slow formation of a white desert.

An image of intense cold is being sought. Its beginnings were explicit in the imagery of the first stanza. In the poet's subconscious mind the card-index of memory is being raked. The conscious, critical faculty is also on the alert—partly as a result of Sue's remark, perhaps—and is ready to select the right image when it presents itself.[2] In the next attempt, we find Emily Dickinson surrendering to the influence of this winter imagery.

[2]   See Dryden (the Preface to *The Rival Ladies*, quoted in *Poetic Process* by George Whalley): 'This worthless present was designed you long before it was a play, when it was only a confused mass of Thoughts, tumbling over one another in the dark; when the Fancy was yet in its first work, moving the sleeping images of things towards the light, there to be distinguished, and then either chosen or rejected by the Judgement'.

Springs—shake the sills—
But—the Echoes—stiffen—
Hoar is the window—
And numb the door—
Tribes—of Eclipse—in Tents—of Marble—
Staples—of Ages—have buckled—there—

There is a return to the house (or palace) image of the first stanza.
Now the house is frost-bound. Outside, the season of spring has
begun, but for the house there will be no thaw. Its *sills, window* and
door are iced-up. Life is over; the long frost-death has begun. The
sensory activity, which within this poem represents life, is no
longer hearing. Now the dead are unable to *feel: And numb the door.*
(There is a vestige of the hearing metaphor in *echoes*; but sound
itself becomes something to touch when the echoes, heard when the
window is rattled by the warming spring wind—another trace of
2a—*stiffen*, like the corpses. The meaning is probably that the dead
are unresponsive to any knock and harden themselves against the
idea of admitting a visitor from the living world of spring.)

Tribes of eclipse reminds us of the historical/universal imagery of 2b.
Here it is used with more success. Generations are seen as nomadic
tribes who live in *tents*, which are not only *marble* in appearance
(stiff, white) but also to the touch. These 'tents' are ice-cold tombs,
and seals are placed on one dying, *eclipsed* generation after another, as
the slabs of the marble tomb are fastened together with *staples*.

The poet is coming closer to finding an objective equivalent for
the imaginative experience of death which had been only partly
realized in 2a and 2b. She knows consciously now that, together with
the ideas of separation and oblivion with which she started, she must
give expression to those of extreme cold and of silence. She also wants
to suggest that the universe, with its great forces, continues inevitably, ignoring the life that it incidentally harbours.

Tribes of eclipse in tents of marble have taken the place of the
planets and the historical images of 2b, but are still not entirely
satisfactory. The ellipsis *tribes of eclipse* (for 'tribes threatened by
eclipse') leads to obscurity, as does the inversion (it is the disappear-
ing generations which have been sealed off in the *tents of marble*). The
intellectual and sensory (visual) elements in this metaphor pull
against each other; there is a rational link between nomadic tribes

and tents; but the tent/tomb identification comes to grief with
staples and buckled; for 'staples' in this context can only be associated
with the marble tomb and 'buckled' only with the nomad's tents.

When Emily Dickinson makes her last attempt at writing a second
stanza, it is interesting to discover that actual phrases, as well as ideas
and images, have begun to take a permanent form. She has been
unable to forget the sound of

> Springs shake the sills
> But the echoes stiffen

and, in the final version, the meaning of these lines is changed with
the least possible dislocation of the word-grouping which her ear
has approved:

> Springs—shake the Seals—
> But the silence—stiffens—
> Frosts unhook—in the Northern Zones—
> Icicles—crawl from Polar Caverns—
> Midnight in Marble—Refutes—the Suns—

The tents of Marble image is the starting point of this revision. The
house image is abandoned, and the stapled tomb becomes a tomb
that has had a metal seal attached to it (signifying the finality of
death). The difficult echoes stiffen is changed to But the silence stiffens:
now we can hear the silence which seems more intense after the
sound of the rattled seals has died away. The image of coldness is
magnified ('Is this frostier?' the poet had asked her critic when she
copied out the previous revision). It is the universe now that is
frost-bound: the ice-cap crawls slowly but inevitably down from
Polar regions to cover all life (the tribes no longer eclipsed, but con-
gealed—the world turning to ice). It is interesting to observe that,
with the expansion of vision in this stanza the appeal to the senses
is multiplied. The first version of the second stanza had appealed
only to the sense of hearing. Now, as well as hearing the rattling
seals, we feel the cold in stiffens, see the slow advance of the glacier in
crawls and, in Midnight in marble refutes the suns, see the total darkness of
the tomb.

It seems strange that, of all the versions of stanza 2, these im-
pressive lines should have been put away, unseen (as far as we know)
by any of her correspondents. Bowles, the newspaper editor, had

received and published the 'Light laughs the breeze' version;
Higginson had been sent 'Grand go the years'; Sue had seen 'Springs
shake the sills'. Only the last version was left, with nearly two
thousand other carefully packeted manuscript poems, to be un-
earthed after her death in 1886. Can we discover a reason for the
poet's decision by examining the poem we should have had if she
had decided to destroy the three previous versions of the second
stanza and unite 'Safe in their alabaster chambers' with 'Springs
shake the seals'?

Safe in their Alabaster Chambers,
Untouched by Morning—
And untouched by Noon—
Sleep the meek members of the Resurrection—
Rafter of Satin—and Roof of Stone—

Springs—shake the Seals—
But the silence—stiffens—
Frosts unhook—in the Northern Zones—
Icicles—crawl from Polar Caverns—
Midnight in Marble—Refutes—the Suns—

Here, the ambiguous *alabaster chambers*, sealed off from the sun,
develop unequivocally into the tomb at the end of the first stanza.
All the misleading hints of rich and secure living (*safe, chambers,
sleep, satin*) of these opening lines are rejected in the second stanza.
Death is final. The tomb is *sealed*. The absence of sunlight (negative)
has become a positive flow of ice, establishing a kingdom of death.
On this side of the grave, spring breezes blow, but they can only
affect the dead by shaking the metal seals on their tombs. Inside the
tomb the irresistible glacier spreads; its marble walls (marble a resolution of alabaster) exclude not just the light of one day's sun, but
of rising and setting suns until the end of time.

Were we right to impose our judgment on Emily Dickinson's and
decide that this is the poem she should have left? Or have we already
discovered the reason for the apparent suppression of what in itself
is a magnificent stanza?

The first stanza achieved its effect by means of understatement and
an ambiguity which at first troubles us and then, as we examine the

apparent contradictions, floods us with intensely cold light (the
'ghostly shimmer' Emily Dickinson's sister-in-law found). The
second presents us with one bold, cosmic image: the whole world
(seen in terms of living generations) is slowly turning to ice.
Perhaps the burden of incompatibility is more than the short,
intense poem can bear. Despite the links of theme and imagery, they
are too far apart. Between the writing of the first and second, a
memorable image has slowly freed itself in the subconscious mind,
but in the process the poem has become broken-backed.

   This was probably the poet's own finding. And so she copied out
the version of 1859 with the original second stanza, and sent it to the
newspaper editor. The suggestion that *cadence* should become plural
(thus making a radical change to the rhythm of its line) was no
doubt his. And on Saturday, 1 March 1862, the poet would have seen
in print (it was one of the mere handful of poems published in her
lifetime):

THE SLEEPING

Safe in their alabaster chambers,
Untouched by morning,
    And untouched by noon,
Sleep the meek members of the Resurrection,
    Rafter of satin, and roof of stone.

Light laughs the breeze
In her castle above them,
    Babbles the bee in a stolid ear,
Pipe the sweet birds in ignorant cadences:
    Ah! What sagacity perished here!

Pelham Hill, June 1861

THE SHAPE

The shape of 'Safe in their Alabaster Chambers' seems to have been
determined at a very early stage in the making of the poem. Although
there was no lack of ideas (as we have seen from the frequent
revisions), and although rigorous condensation of the material led

to obscurity in some of the revisions, Emily Dickinson kept to her original intention. The poem was to consist of two short stanzas, and was made like a hinge, the meeting point of the two plates being that abandoning of euphemism that we noticed at the end of the first stanza.

The shape of Wilfred Owen's 'Miners' could well have been suggested by the actual conditions which inspired the imaginative experience which his poem reflects. Owen was on sick leave from the Belgian front when he wrote this poem in January 1918. Convalescing in Scarborough, he had been disturbed by the sight of holiday-makers on the sands; the gap between their apparently carefree world, and the sphere of squalid suffering, less than two hundred miles away, which he was unable to forget, was too wide to be bridged. That January, he might well have sat by a fire like the one he describes in the poem, and found his thoughts wandering inevitably back to the horrors of trench warfare which he was soon to experience again. The poem is a bitter reflection on the ingratitude (through ignorance) of those who were benefiting, or would benefit, from that sacrifice.

MINERS

There was a whispering in my hearth,
   A sigh of the coal,
Grown wistful of a former earth
   It might recall.

I listened for a tale of leaves
   And smothered ferns;
Frond-forests; and the low, sly lives
   Before the fawns.

My fire might show steam-phantoms simmer
   From Time's old cauldron,
Before the birds made nests in summer,
   Or men had children.

But the coals were murmuring of their mine,
   And moans down there
Of boys that slept wry sleep, and men
   Writhing for air.

And I saw white bones in the cinder-shard.
  Bones without number;
For many hearts with coal are charred
  And few remember.

I thought of some who worked dark pits
  Of war, and died
Digging the rock where Death reputes
  Peace lies indeed.

Comforted years will sit soft-chaired
  In rooms of amber;
The years will stretch their hands, well-cheered
  By our lives' ember.

The centuries will burn rich loads
  With which we groaned,
Whose warmth shall lull their dreaming lids
  While songs are crooned.
But they will not dream of us poor lads
  Lost in the ground.

The heart of the experience is the contrast between the trenches
and the fire-lit room. A metaphor which identifies soldiers ('mining'
for peace in Flanders clay) with coal-miners provides the necessary
bridge. Coal has the obvious association of hearth and home;
mining brings with it the idea of pit disasters and sacrificed lives.
But because Wilfred Owen wishes to recapture that original state of
alienation which he had experienced amongst the holiday-makers, he
must treat the metaphor circumspectly, lull his readers (after a
deliberately misleading title) into a false state of security. Their
thoughts must be as far away from the battlefield as the thoughts of
the people on Scarborough sands; and then, suddenly, they must
be forced to recollect themselves.

In keeping with the warmth and security of the fireside scene they
present, the first three stanzas are quiet and gently fanciful. Does the
escaping gas want to tell the poet something about the prehistoric
forests that coal was formed from? The shape and rhythm of the
quatrains that lead us reflectively from one notion to another help
to create an atmosphere of warmth, idleness and ease. The short

lines, each causing a break in the rhythmic flow of the verse, suggest placid, perhaps disjointed reflection. The poem seems loosely structured; it appears to meander from stanza to stanza, from one fancy to another.

The first turning-point comes in stanza four:

> But the coals were murmuring of their mine

The uncertain 'might recall', 'Might show' have developed into the positive 'were murmuring'. Conjectured fawns and prehistoric birds give place to historical mine disasters and child labour. This second movement comes to a climax with the grim and intentionally ambiguous

> For many hearts with coal are charred
> And few remember

And here, rather than in the artificially built up train of reflection that has preceded it, we sense the germ of the poem: the shocked realization of the convalescing soldier that few really care and fewer will remember.

The foregoing stanzas were deceptive. They have led us, like the slowly converging walls of a trap, to a point of recognition. And the next lines

> I thought of some who worked dark pits
> Of war . . .

reveal that everything that has led up to them is an extended metaphor. The poem is not about life in the mines, but about trench warfare; not about miners involved in pit disasters, but soldiers involved in the disaster of war. It is the one word war (line 22) which shows that the stanzas we accepted as literal were actually figurative. Owen has given a practical demonstration of our own forgetfulness. By the comfortable fireside we have been content to dream idly about prehistory. Only by chance, as we followed the flow of conjecture, did we realize our debt to the miners; and it is only by this process, in an idle, comfortable moment, that we recall the other debt. And, after a single hint at that, Owen points our guilt, not by abandoning his metaphor and describing the trenches, but by transporting us back to the comfortable room, now described with great sensuousness:

> Comforted years will sit soft-chaired
> In rooms of amber

Now, the idea of wasted lives, which in stanza 5 had seemed to refer to the miners, is clearly transferred to Owen's fellow-soldiers: for the first time in the poem, the second person plural, *our*, is used:

> The years will stretch their hands, well-cheered
>   By our lives' ember.

And in the final stanza, by means of the same metaphor, the ideas of comfort and the suffering that has secured it are fused:

> The centuries will burn rich loads
>   With which we groaned,
> Whose warmth shall lull their dreaming lids
>   While songs are crooned.

Finally, the metaphor is abandoned. Instead of ending with the quatrain, as we expect him to, Owen extends the stanza and leaves us with a blunt postscript:

> But they will not dream of us poor lads
>   Lost in the ground.

A poem which has had the deceptively simple and engaging appearance of a series of stanzas strung together to accommodate a gently meandering reverie has proved to be the embodiment of a carefully defined experience and, in Valéry's metaphor, an efficient 'machine' for stimulating a response in us, the readers, and giving us the opportunity to re-create that experience for ourselves.

METAPHORS AND SYMBOLS

'Death is terrible to us because it marks the end of sensory experience.' It would be possible, though perhaps not much to our taste, to write down a mathematical equation in which Emily Dickinson's poem, 'Safe in their Alabaster Chambers' (D) was represented as the equivalent in poetry of a prose abstract (G):

$$D \times Prose = G \times Poetry$$

The unknown quantities, capable of maintaining this unlikely balance are, of course, Prose and Poetry. What basic difference in approach to the raw material of experience is implied by these two words?

Wanting to express her particular imaginative experience of death,

Emily Dickinson, in her final revision of the troublesome second stanza, presents us with a picture—a picture which obviously doesn't reflect anything real in the external world, but which has come to being in her imagination and is made up of so many items of her everyday experience: spring; a sealed marble tomb (perhaps seen at Pelham Hills); frost and icicles; an encyclopedia article about the Arctic; the sun; night. None of these elements is very remarkable in itself; but of course in this stanza we don't normally see them as 'elements' or 'items' at all. We respond to a single picture and if the poem succeeds with us, we find in it an embodiment of the imaginative event for which the rather dreary transcript above has been offered as an 'equivalent'. Expressing this idea differently and using a dangerous and potentially misleading word— but one which is part of our heritage in literary criticism—we might say that in her second stanza Emily Dickinson had created a poetic 'image'.

Sir Philip Sidney used this word in its modern sense in the *Apologie for Poetrie* when, comparing the poet with the philosopher, he wrote: '[the poet] yieldeth to the powers of the mind an image of that whereof the Philosopher bestoweth but a woordish description'.

Although Sidney goes on to identify 'image' almost exclusively with the classical human types (Ajax providing us with an 'image' of anger, for instance), the embryo of subsequent critical theory lies there. Applied to the Emily Dickinson poem, the 'woordish description' is the prose abstract; the 'image' is the picture of the tomb in its polar landscape.

Grounds for caution in the use of this word may already have been noticed. It so happens that Emily Dickinson's image *is* a picture (and of course this *often* happens in the writing of poetry, since many of us think and feel in terms of pictures); but the Ajax 'image' that Sidney referred to was not necessarily pictorial. Our ability, in that case, to respond fully to the concept 'anger' would depend less on our having a clear notion of what Ajax *looked* like, than on our memories, if any, of what happened in the Ajax episodes of *The Iliad*. Similarly, if we go back to an earlier version of Emily Dickinson's second stanza, we find her expressing the idea of the passing of time, and hence mortality, in an 'image' which has strong non-visual elements:

> Diadems fall and Doges surrender.

(Here we might perhaps arrive at her idea through the picture of a crown struck from a monarch's head; but we are more likely to by-pass the strictly visual and think in more general historical terms of political murder and revolution.[3]

Far from being synonymous with 'picture', therefore, the poetic image may be non-sensory ('Doges surrender'), or appeal, apart from the eyes, to memories of things smelt and tasted, heard or touched or, more rarely, to the sense of motion.[4] Emily Dickinson's 'But the echoes stiffen' appeals to the senses of hearing and touch, but not at all to the eyes.

We may arrive at an answer to that deceptively simple question, and determine the essential difference between poetry and prose if we remember again the assortment of items that went to the making of Emily Dickinson's 'polar ice' image. If these five lines had been preserved only as a fragment torn from its context, the seals, the spring, the north pole and graveyard would have formed a striking, but obscure and enigmatic description. But in their context all these items have coalesced to give us the poet's experience of death. If we give the poem a fair chance, we relax, leave ourselves open to the series of concepts that are offered us: spring, seals, silence, stiffness, frost, icicles, crawling arctic ice, midnight, the sun, time. There is no difficulty here. Each allusion invites a response from our own experience; and to absorb meaning from the lines we have only to allow our-selves to respond. We must discard our prose-approach to reading, with its emphasis on analysis, relationship and logical progression;

[3] A corollary of the fact that not all poetic images are pictures is that not all pictures in poetry are images in the strict, and critically useful sense. For example, in a celebrated passage from Milton's Lycidas:

Bring the rath Primrose that forsaken dies.
The tufted Crow-toe, and pale Gessamine,
The white Pink, and the Pansie freakt with jeat,
The glowing Violet.
The musk-rose, and the well attir'd Woodbine.
With Cowslips wan that hang the pensive hed . . .

the flowers are there for their own sakes; and it would be more accurate to describe them as part of the pictorial and sensuous content of the poem rather than as its 'imagery'.
[4] kinaesthetic images, e.g. G. M. Hopkins's portrayal of the Windhover's flight in the lines:

. . . in his riding
Of the rolling level underneath him steady air

put our trust in the poet, and liberate ourselves to the various elements of her image. In this way we may arrive at the goal of all poetry-reading and re-create for ourselves, out of the material offered, a poetic event.

Reduced to the simplest statement then: Whereas in prose, we follow a reasoned argument, the tools of grammar and syntax having been used to analyse and to illustrate relationships (consider the role of conjunctions like but, although, if), in poetry, we are invited to immerse ourselves in a flow of 'images'; we are asked to explore the memories, sensory or intellectual, which they awaken, and to reorganize these memories along lines suggested by the way in which the images act on each other. The result is that we share a poetic experience, apprehending the quality of the poet's feeling.[5]

It might still be asked: 'Why does the poet have to communicate in this special, and possibly obscure, way?' We could find an answer to this by considering the language we use. This is an excellent means of communicating relationship and the distinctions to be drawn between one concept and another. Writing about a walk through the park, we have no difficulty in defining exactly what we have seen—tree, elm, oak, bush, flowering-shrub, etc.: each distinguishing name has its accompanying picture; and we might distinguish further by adding an adjective (tall, yellow), or a phrase (by the river, near the gate). But, so far, the relationship between the tree and the person looking at the tree has been left out; and, when we try to define that, we run into difficulties. Conventional terms certainly exist. We might write: 'I saw a beautiful tree in the park this morning'; or 'What a marvellous colour that almond blossom is!' But we may feel that these ready-made forms haven't really done justice to the particular quality of our experience. (The question of decorum occurs here. How often do we limit ourselves to a mere 'How nice!' from fear of striking the wrong note in a conversation or

---

[5] This is a basic distinction, and attempts nothing more subtle than to pinpoint the difference between the Plowden Report and The Tempest. We are concerned with creative writing and therefore with a distinction between the prosaic and the poetic. There is no intention of suggesting that it is possible to draw a distinct dividing line between Poetry and Prose. If we did, no doubt Ulysses and The Vanity of Human Wishes would find themselves on the wrong side of it. It was Molière's M. Jourdain whose literary studies began and ended with the dazzled realization that he had been talking Prose all his life; and perhaps we should take warning from that.

a letter?) In the following lines, a poet—Gerard Manley Hopkins—
expresses his feelings about some poplars that have been cut down:

My aspens dear, whose airy cages quelled,
Quelled or quenched in leaves the leaping sun,
All felled, felled, are all felled;
  Of a fresh and following folded rank
    Not spared, not one . . .

Here the diction and rhythm of the lines tell us about far more than
the trees themselves. Accompanying the protest is the reason for it:
the poet's involvement with the objects he describes.

In the act of creating, the poet never retreats from feeling, as we
obviously do when we select the word 'nice'. At such a moment,
reality for him is feeling: and the particular relief for which the act
of creation is a search is to understand that feeling and to discover a
formula which will allow him to build up, piece by piece, outside
himself, the experience from which the feeling has sprung.[6] This
formula is the poem. And we in turn build up the original experience
when we interpret that formula.

Shelley's concept of the poet as a 'legislator' and 'messenger'
who communicates messages to mankind from an 'ethereal world'
merges into one of a musician playing a lyre—the lyre being us,
the readers. Poets, in Shelley's metaphor, 'touch the enchanted chord'
and reanimate in the reader 'the sleeping, the cold, the buried
images of the past'. Sensations (messages received by the senses)
or memories, stored away at moments when our feelings have been
engaged, are a common possession of both reader and poet. When
the right string is plucked, they are awoken and placed at the service
of the poet.

But how does the poet's memory operate? Sometimes his search
for an image is fully conscious. Wordsworth may have been thinking
of this when he wrote of 'emotion recollected in tranquillity': a
feeling is recalled; this effort of the memory forces up the now

---

[6]   T. S. Eliot's term 'objective correlative' expresses this function: the poet
finds an objective equivalent in words, images, rhythm and form for what
must be in origin a subjective experience. If he succeeds, the experience
encased in the 'objective correlative' becomes available to anyone who is
willing to expose himself to the influence of the poem.

buried impressions which once accompanied that feeling; and they become the images of the poem. Sometimes they present themselves unasked—many of the dream images of The Rime of the Ancient Mariner are of this kind. More often, perhaps, the will and the unconscious mind work together, as in the case of the Emily Dickinson poem. An image was needed; it suggested itself first in the phrase untouched by morning and again in Silent as dots on a disc of snow; was examined critically (the note to Sue—'Is this frostier?'); and expanded into the arctic image of the final version. Yeats, describing this process, wrote: 'One must allow the images to form with all their associations before one criticises . . . bring up from the unconscious anything you already possess a fragment of.'[7] And in this he was echoing Dryden, whose metaphor for poetic creation, as we have seen, was of the 'Fancy . . . moving the sleeping images of things towards the light'.

Feelings appear to attach themselves naturally to sense impressions, and vice versa. We all have our own examples. The smell of a certain kind of soap may remind us of long-forgotten feelings about someone we once knew, or about a certain phase of our lives. And the corollary of this phenomenon is that, once a poet has recalled the feeling, he may be able to describe with great accuracy the accompanying sense-impressions that he absorbed at that time and in that place. A vague 'feeling' is then rooted in sensory experience: the spiritual state expressed poetically in the vocabulary of seeing, hearing, tasting, smelling, touching. Sense-impressions are the valid currency of poetic experience and the means by which it is communicated.

In the description of Alisoun in Chaucer's 'Miller's Tale', we find an example of a poet's attempt to tap a reserve of feeling in us by referring to an object which is likely to prove a meeting point between his own inner experience and ours. At the same time we see the poetic image in its rudimentary and easily recognizable form, the simile.

Ful smale ypulled were hire browes two,
And tho were bent and blake as any sloo.
She was ful moore blisful on to see
Than is the newe pere-jonette tree . . .

The comparison drawn between Alisoun and the pear tree tells us

[7] Quoted by George Whalley in Poetic Process.

very little about the girl's appearance (unlike the 'sloe' simile) but we are invited to transfer whatever feelings of enthusiasm the sight of pear blossom might have kindled in us to Alisoun, and in this way participate in Chaucer's feelings about her.

In the comparison between arching black eyebrows and sloes, our instinctive tendency to search for harmony is satisfied by the exactness of the parallel. (Bacon wrote of similes: 'Neither are these only similitudes . . . but the same footsteps of nature, treading and printing upon several subjects or matters'. As the movement of the planets might be seen as a cosmic reflection of the circling of electrons round the nucleus of an atom.) Chaucer's sloe simile, besides satisfying us by the exactness of the parallel it draws, gives us a clearer picture of Alisoun, and (taken with a series of animal and plant metaphors in this portrait) provides a third dimension of earthiness and natural vigour to the list of her charms.

The 'pere-jonette' comparison is perhaps more interesting because, by modern standards, its appeal has a simplicity that approaches the naive. We take it on trust. Writing like this today, we might be accused of taking our readers' response too much for granted. Byron, describing his Juan washed up half-dead on a beach, and

> Droop'd as the willow when no winds can breathe

was mocking this kind of simile (and deliberately allowing his own to give the opposite picture to the one we should have had):

And she bent o'er him, and he lay beneath,
Hush'd as the babe upon its mother's breast,
Droop'd as the willow when no winds can breathe,
Lull'd like the depth of ocean when at rest,
Fair as the crowning rose of the whole wreath,
Soft as the callow cygnet in its nest;
In short, he was a very pretty fellow,
Although his woes had turn'd him rather yellow.

The danger that Byron satirically underlines is the total disappearance of the intellectual element from a comparison. Ideally, a simile or metaphor should be evocative, create resonance, inspire us to transfer feeling from a remembered sensation of our own to the new experience for which the poem is a formula. But there are other

requirements for an effective comparison. The reason, perceiving
hidden relationships, should ensure that it is *accurate*. And the poet's
desire to establish a certain mood will lead to the search for a
comparison which is *appropriate* to his intention and in harmony with
the other images. Byron's willow simile invites the unsuspecting
reader to do the poet's work for him, and to bring to the beach
scene any feelings that have already been stimulated by other willow
references in literature; he is then shown his error, unkindly
perhaps, in the bathetic concluding couplet.

Banquo's address to the witches in the first act of *Macbeth* provides
us with an illustration of a more serious use of metaphor in poetry

> I'th'name of truth,
> Are ye fantastical, or that indeed
> Which outwardly ye show? My noble partner
> You greet with present grace, and great prediction
> Of noble having, and of royal hope,
> That he seems rapt withal: to me you speak not.
> *If you can look into the seeds of time,*
> *And say which grain will grow, and which will not,*
> Speak then to me, who neither beg, nor fear,
> Your favours nor your hate.

It is when we try to reduce the speech to a prose abstract that we
discover the importance of the *seeds of time* metaphor. For here
imagery is no longer merely supporting meaning: it is actually
conveying it. It would be very difficult to express Banquo's thought
without the image in which it is embodied.

The witches can foresee events in the future. In terms of the
metaphor, these events are plants. Since an event is a last link in a
chain of personalities, ideas, words and actions, an idea coming into
the mind of a certain man at a certain time may be to some future
event what the seed is to the plant. But some ideas remain buried:
not all seeds grow. It is at this point that we begin to appreciate the
need for metaphor. That seeds grow into plants is a commonplace
of our own experience. By analogy, we see that any event is a
culminating point in a series, but it is not always possible to define
the nature of that series, or to say what its starting point has been.
The murder of Duncan follows the temptation offered Macbeth by

the witches' prophecy, his wife's ambition, and the unlucky opportunity given by Duncan's visit to Glamis. But what lies beyond these? From what event, psychological or supernatural, does Macbeth's own ambition spring? We go back as far as we can, but eventually, as in all attempts to find the mainspring of human action, we find ourselves confronted by a wall: a mystery as imponderable as that suggested by the insignificant but powerful seed.

When Wordsworth uses the same metaphor in 'To a Highland Girl', we again have the feeling that a poet has come face to face with a mystery and found that the language of reason is no longer of use. The statements of poetry are different from the statements of prose; and metaphor, when all its resources are brought into play, is a mode of expression, not an extraneous ornament, as it might become in the kind of poetry that Byron mocked.

. . . With earnest feeling I shall pray
For thee when I am far away:
For never saw I mien, or face,
In which more plainly I could trace
Benignity and home-bred sense
Ripening in perfect innocence.
Here, scatter'd like a random seed,
Remote from men, Thou doest not need
The embarrass'd look of shy distress,
And maidenly shamefacedness:
Thou wear'st upon thy forehead clear
The freedom of a Mountaineer.

It is as difficult to find a prose equivalent for ripening as it was for seeds of time. The metaphor carries us beyond the limits that would have been set by prose and allows us to absorb the idea of the continuous but unobserved growth which transforms the girl's face into a woman's.

The seed metaphor also acts as a conductor for the particular feelings that the sight of the highland girl has inspired in the poet. Feelings relating to incorrupt nature, fertility and wholesomeness are brought into play, perhaps below the level of consciousness. Above all we sense the mystery of change and growth. A spark jumps a gap and these feelings are transferred to the girl. The reader shares something of the poet's awe as he contemplates her growing into womanhood.

Like Shakespeare, Wordsworth uses metaphor to extend his meaning and to suggest his own involvement in a poetic event.

But if we have kept 'Safe in their Alabaster Chambers' in mind throughout this discussion of poetic imagery, we may feel that the images so far discussed are quite different in kind from the composite picture in the second stanza of that poem.

Springs shake the Seals—
But the silence stiffens—
Frosts unhook in the Northern Zones—
Icicles crawl from Polar Caverns—
Midnight in Marble Refutes the Suns.

There is an arbitrary, private quality about this which makes analysis comparatively difficult (although, as we have seen, the actual *idea* embodied in it is a simple one). In contrast, Shakespeare and Wordsworth, expressing far more complex ideas, have chosen a metaphor (seed, growth) whose elements are simple and readily accessible to us. Emily Dickinson's image could exist, though puzzlingly, in its own right, detached from its context; but the seed metaphors are an integral part of the poetic statement as a whole and couldn't be detached in this way. For these reasons we are unable to apply the term metaphor to the polar-ice image; and must use a different term: symbol.

The point of departure for symbols may be seen if we look at two passages, the first from Keats's 'Isabella' and the second from Yeats's 'The Secret Rose'.

Parting they seem'd to tread upon the air,
    Twin roses by the zephyr blown apart
Only to meet again more close, and share
    The inward fragrance of each other's heart.
She, to her chamber gone, a ditty fair
    Sang, of delicious love and honey'd dart;
He with light steps went up a western hill,
And bade the sun farewell, and joy'd his fill.

—Keats, wishing to establish Isabella and Lorenzo in our imagination

as a pair of ideal lovers, invites us to draw from our stock of remembered sensations the rose's colour, shape and scent, as well as
the tradition (well established in poetry) that the rose represents
perfection. At a glance, it might seem that this is the kind of invitation Byron was warning us about. But this is unfair to Keats, who has
visualized these roses. For him, the two growing on one stalk but
momentarily blown apart by the wind really represents the spiritu-
ally united but physically separate lovers (just as 'stiff twin com-
passes' did for Donne). And through the allusion to the roses' scent
is expressed the idea of the lovers perceiving qualities in each other
which they are unable to define:

> The inward fragrance of each other's heart

—As in Shakespeare's and Wordsworth's seed images, the figurative
meaning at this point extends beyond the reach of the literal meaning. But, as with those metaphors, Keats's image of the roses is
entirely at the service of an idea.

When we turn to Yeats's lines, our first sensation is that we have
been knocked off our feet almost as soon as entering the water and
carried out of our depth.

Far-off, most secret, and inviolate Rose,
Enfold me in my hour of hours; where those
Who sought thee in the Holy Sepulchre,
Or in the wine-vat, dwell beyond the stir
And tumult of defeated dreams; and deep
Among pale eyelids, heavy with the sleep
Men have named beauty. Thy great leaves enfold
The ancient beards, the helms of ruby and gold
Of the crowned Magi; and the king whose eyes
Saw the Pierced Hands and Rood of elder rise
In Druid vapour and make the torches dim . . .

We sense that Yeats's Rose is not just a rose, and that we have
entered a private domain of imaginative experience; where Keats's
twin roses were an image in a poem, this Rose is the poem. Similarly,
we may have felt that when Emily Dickinson had arrived at her
remarkable picture in the last version of her second stanza, her
object in writing 'Safe in their Alabaster Chambers' had finally been
achieved.

In Yeats's poem we feel the autonomy of the Rose image, an independence of its context which shows it to be a symbol. References to the birth and passion of Christ (the Magi, the Pierced Hands and the Rood of elder, the wine-vat, the Holy Sepulchre) hint at a mystic experience; but there is an apparent lack of consideration for any intellectual need of the reader to attach the Rose to an idea. Apart from the above pointers, the reason is bypassed. We are thrown back on our senses. The word *enfold* (lines 2 and 7) directs us to a particular physical property of the Rose: fold on fold of inter-leaved petals arching over a central cluster of stamens. Until this picture is captured by the inner eye, we remain outside Yeats's experience.

The Rose symbolizes a state of mystic communion in which the rational subject–object distinction breaks down. The contemplater becomes part of the Contemplated. *Far-off, most secret and inviolate* seem to identify the Rose with the Contemplated. *Enfold me in my hour of hours* anticipates the poet's entry into the trance state outside time, and seems to identify the traditionally most-beautiful flower with the state of communion which is the pinnacle of all experience. The form of the Rose suggests something hidden in the midst of physical beauty: the ultimate goal, the ideal, permanent beauty which Words-worth sensed while contemplating a child or flowers, and Keats in the song of a nightingale or a Greek vase.

In a symbol, one meaning can overlap another. The relationship between certain ideas and the pere-jonette, or seed or twin-roses images was clearly expressed. Here, no boundaries are defined. At one moment, Yeats's Rose appears to be the Contemplated; in the next (*Enfold me* following closely on *secret* and *inviolate*), it becomes the state of contemplation, when the mystic becomes part of what he contemplates. The Rose is no longer the Contemplated, but has become the moment out of time when the contemplater is caught up, lifted out of his temporal existence, wrapped round protectively as if within the petals of the Rose.

THE WORDS

We have probably all responded at one time or another to a poem like the sonnet that follows. Some of us will have tried to write in

this vein, though we may have fallen well short of the technical
competence it displays.

All perfect things are saddening in effect.
The autumn wood robed in its scarlet clothes,
The matchless tinting on the royal rose
Whose velvet leaf by no least flaw is flecked;
Love's supreme moment, when the soul unchecked
Soars high as heaven, and its best rapture knows,
These hold a deeper pathos than our woes,
Since they leave nothing better to expect.

Resistless change, when powerless to improve,
Can only mar. The gold will pale to grey—
No thing remains tomorrow as today—
The rose will not seem quite so fair, and love
Must find its measures of delight made less.
Ah, how imperfect is all Perfectness!

Coming back to such verse after reading Emily Dickinson or
Wilfred Owen, we may sense its inadequacy without being able to
formulate our dissatisfaction. Words like 'over-ripe' or 'sentimental'
might come to mind: but how to prove our point? And how, if we
are writers too, to learn from another performer's mistakes?

In our uncertainty we might pause in the first place at two or three
words, e.g. 'perfect', 'supreme', 'rapture'. Aren't they a little tired?
Haven't they been the 'establishment' words for a certain kind of
poetic expression for too long? If we have ever responded to the
invitation they offer, we may begin now to distrust them and to
suspect that in the past we have committed ourselves too soon and
too easily—in any case before the poet has proved to us that he or
she has a valid experience to offer.

This questioning of the use of words is a good beginning for the
criticism of a poem. In fact we should be participating in that endless
debate of which Wordsworth's brave overstatements in the Preface
to the Lyrical Ballads and Dr Johnson's dislike of the opening lines of
Lycidas or 'the blanket of the dark', and Shakespeare's mockery of
dramatic styles in the Players' scenes of Hamlet are all a part. The
question which is repeatedly asked is 'What is the true language of
poetry?'

Coleridge's definition of poetry was 'the best words in the best order'. We might gloss 'best words' as words which not only match the sense by conveying the raw idea, but which also convey the writer's feeling about that idea, and perhaps, if the linguistic resources are available, suggest a relationship between the idea and the sounds that embody it. If we were writing a poem in which we wanted to allude to the noise produced by a colony of bees, we should be able to choose, for example, from amongst such words as *buzzing*, *humming*, *droning* or *murmuring*, according to our sensory alertness to the actual quality of the sound, and to our feelings about it (whether or not we liked it); and we might feel that there was an echo of the actual sound of the swarm in the word we had chosen.

We might try to resolve our uncertainty about 'Perfection' by asking if this poet has used 'the best words', always bearing in mind that there are two parts to this question: *a*) Has she found the exact word to convey her idea and the nuances of feeling attached to it; and—using the other end of the telescope—*b*) Has the word been used with a full consciousness of its potential meaning for us, the readers; and are meanings which we are likely to bring to bear on it catered for within the context?

This is an ambitious poem because it professes to deal with absolute qualities. The play on 'perfect', 'imperfect', 'Perfectness' seems to hold out the promise that it will give us a poetic experience of the concept 'Perfection' (as Keats did in his Platonic 'Ode on a Grecian Urn'). The last line, in particular, has the air of having explored a philosophical concept and expressed it in a triumphant paradox (as a poet of the Metaphysical school might have done). But the poet's intellect is not her strongest point, and when we look for an equivalent in poetry of that concept 'perfection', we find only random impressions, 'the autumn wood', 'the royal rose', 'Love's supreme moment', which in appealing direct to the feelings attempt to bypass the intellect altogether.

While 'perfection' is allowed to float, meaningless and unmoored, the superlatives, *matchless*, *supreme* and *best* are equally meaningless as we have no standard to refer them to; and in the absence of such a standard, we begin to suspect that, through these apparently highly charged, but actually empty, words, the poet is communicating the illusion of an experience rather than actual objectified feeling.

The tautology in the second line adds to the impression that a slender poem has been excessively inflated. On close examination, one of the terms of the royal robes metaphor is found to be unnecessary: must the autumn leaves be described as both *clothes* and *robes*? And should a rose-*petal* be described as a *leaf*?

This inability to match up to the full potential of the words used, which makes 'Perfection' disappointing as a philosophical poem, is reflected in a lack of awareness in the other direction. The colloquial use of *in effect* ('In effect you are saying. . . .') has been overlooked; and, whereas the sense demands an expansion of this ellipsis into 'in the effect they have on us', the popular usage pulls us hard in the other direction. The short-hand of the colloquial has probably been used consciously in *quite so*; but the result is a retreat into the evasions of everyday speech, away from that precision about feeling which we expect from poetry.

Our suspicions about 'Perfection' will very probably be confirmed by the obvious affectation of *No thing*. Of course, if the meaning of *nothing* could have been affected by its change into this unorthodox form, the poet would have been perfectly justified in coining the new phrase. But in the absence of the new dimension which it leads us to expect, we again feel that the poet is going through the motions of communicating an experience without having anything genuine to offer.

In the four extracts that follow, certain words and phrases have been selected for special attention. In each case, the same question will be asked: 'Should the poet be using words in this way?'

(1)

But when the melancholy fit shall fall
Sudden from heaven like a weeping cloud,
That fosters the *droop-headed* flowers all,
And hides the green hill in an April shroud;
Then *glut* thy sorrow on a morning rose,
Or on the rainbow of the salt *sand-wave*,
Or on the *wealth* of globed peonies;
Or if thy mistress some *rich* anger shows,
Emprison her soft hand, and let her rave,
And feed deep, deep upon her peerless eyes.

Here, fit might stop us for a moment, until we see that behind the colloquialism there may lie a deliberate allusion to disease, which is quite appropriate in the context. And the very use of a colloquial rather than a clinical word to suggest the seizure 'sudden from heaven' helps to keep the allusion in its place—a suggestion rather than a dominant chord.

The coinings, the compound words, droop-headed and sand-wave, can also be justified since they contain necessary pictures which no existing words could convey. Sand-wave is more elliptical than droop-headed, and it does tend towards obscurity; but if we allow rainbow and salt full play we arrive at a picture: ripples of sand at low tide which have retained salt and become iridescent.

Do glut and feed strike discordant notes? Glut stands out amongst words like April, shroud, sorrow and rose; feed next to deep and peerless. These two linked words seem to have been used deliberately: they form a single metaphor which at first seems strange in a poem about melancholy. But the emotional-hunger/physical-hunger parallel that it suggests is a valid one; and the final line is skilfully contrived to make the image acceptable. The repeated deep after feed makes us think of the contemplated eyes rather than the act of eating. As in the case of fit, the image has been muted so that we only become fully conscious of it when we subject the lines to analysis. The image suggested by wealth and rich develops naturally from the idea of the lavish and abundant Nature implied in the allusions to the nourishing rain-cloud (fosters) and the brilliance of the rose and the rainbow-like sand.

Unlike perfect and supreme in 'Perfection', the hyperbolic peerless is planted in well-prepared ground. The idea of an abundance of beautiful things has already been established. The stanza has the form of a crescendo: the green hill, spring rain, the fresh rose, the iridescent beach, the peonies, the beautiful woman. Anything short of peerless would be an anticlimax: the mistress who has been placed on this pedestal of lesser beauties must have the most beautiful eyes in the world.

(2)

Let the mad poets say whate'er they please
Of the sweets of Faeries, Peris, Goddesses,

There is not such a *treat* among them all,
Haunters of cavern, lake and waterfall,
As a *real* woman, lineal *indeed*
From Pyrrha's pebbles or old Adam's seed.
Thus gentle Lamia judg'd, *and judg'd aright*,
That Lycius could not love *in half a fright* . . .

Tiring for a moment, in a long narrative poem, the poet allows *treat* to evade his critical vigilance. The proximity of *sweets* (line 2) suggests that an eating metaphor is intended (as in 1); but the general usage at the time when these lines were written allowed the slight shift of meaning which we are familiar with. An OED entry for 1825 gives: 'Lord Dudley is a treat, and deserves his cutlets for the admirable despatch he wrote'. There is nothing in these lines to suggest the poet's awareness of the way in which the word has degenerated; and his own meaning floats uneasily between the eating metaphor (used much less successfully here than in 1) and the colloquialism. The displeasing sweet/treat jingle must also be noticed.

The treat offered for consumption is a *real* woman; and although the situation described actually demands a distinction between a real and an *unreal* (i.e. phantasmal) woman, the memory of the debased usage of prose ('He is the real thing and no mistake'—OED entry for 1818) is too strong: we expect the colloquial rather than the philosophical usage of *real*, especially after the careless *treat*. As with *in effect* in 'Perfection', the popular usage has made the serious use of the word very much more difficult; and in these cases, neither poet has been able to cancel out our memory of the more familiar context.

A different reminder of everyday speech comes from the adapted repetition *and judg'd aright* ('he argued the point, and argued it well'). Here the tone of the line is affected in a curious way: a jovial, almost hearty note is struck, quite out of key with the prevailing mood of the passage. The tone veers again with *in half a fright*. Aiming at lightness, the poet has chosen words which give instead the impression of jocularity.

Having rejected, by implication, the belief that a special kind of language has been hallowed and made sacrosanct for future poetic usage (e.g. words like *rapture* and *supreme*), must we also reject the

Wordsworthian dictum that the true language of poetry is 'the language of men'?—In its extreme form, yes. Wordsworth over-stated his case; and overlooked the fact that the 'real language of men' was quite likely to be the kind of slipshod diction which crept into the lines from 'Lamia'. In 3, however, Pope shows us how even slang can be given poetic validity. The necessary ingredient for success is awareness.

(3)

Rufa, whose eye quick-glancing o'er the Park,
Attracts each light gay meteor of a *Spark*,
Agrees as ill with Rufa studying Locke,
As Sappho's di'monds with her *dirty smock*;
Or Sappho at her toilet's *greasy task*,
With Sappho fragrant at an ev'ning Mask:
So morning Insects that in muck begun,
Shine, *buzz* and *fly-blow* in the setting sun.

This is the kind of passage which provokes the perennial question: Can satire be poetry? We are immediately struck by the 'low' register of *dirty smock, greasy task, muck, fly-blow* and *buzz*; and even if we avoid the fallacy that poetry deals only with the sweet or noble, we may want to protest, at first encounter, that these lines demonstrate a fundamentally unpoetic approach to language; are clever versifica-tion rather than poetry.

As we saw in 2, slang used carelessly must be unpoetic. But in these lines, *Spark*, an eighteenth-century term for 'playboy', is deliberately held up for us to examine. In itself, the slang word is metaphorical: a playboy—showy, superficial—is like a brilliant, self-consuming, short-lived flame. A neat value-judgment is made by means of the pathetic placing of *spark* after *meteor*. (Further, if we visualize the spark metaphor, we find a reflection of the glint in Rufa's roving eye— which is elsewhere recalled in the twinkle of Sappho's diamonds (line 4) and the dying light that is flashed momentarily from the insects at sunset (line 8).)

The 'low' phrase *dirty smock* is similarly used with great care. The unexpected coupling in rhyme of the philosopher with Sappho's unwashed clothes is designed to make us aware—with a shock—of

Rufa's fragmented, unbalanced personality. Other 'low' words are selected for their power of suggestion; sound and sense being closely related in *greasy* and *buzz*, and *muck* placed in the line where it receives maximum stress and conveys the poet's feeling of disgust. *Fly-blow*, balanced against *shine* and *setting sun*, gives another poetic 'shock'.

In this case, the analysis of the poet's diction, coupled with our sense of the strength of feeling reflected in the lines, may persuade us that this is poetry, even if the dominant feeling—disgust—is one that poetry embodies only very rarely.

(4)

Into the snows she sweeps,
Hurling the haven behind,
The Deutschland, on Sunday; and so the sky *keeps*,
For the infinite air is *unkind*,
And the sea flint-flake, black backed in *the regular blow*,
Sitting Eastnortheast, in cursed quarter, the wind;
Wiry and white-fiery and whirlwind-swivelled snow
Spins to the *widow-making unchilding unfathering* deeps.

Again, the question of unconventional usage is raised. *Keeps* has the sense 'continues' (rather as it would be used in 'Are you keeping well?'); a noun, *blow*, has been coined out of a verb, for 'the blowing of the wind'; *sitting* has the meaning 'blowing from'. In his use of these semi-nautical terms, Gerard Manley Hopkins seems to remind us of the way in which the sailors and travellers would have talked about the storm which eventually destroys their ship.

Through *unkind*, we are reminded of another colloquialism ('the weather was unkind to us'); but such a usage is obviously out of keeping with the adjective *infinite* applied to the same noun, *air*; for this gives the storm a cosmic setting. Whilst acknowledging the colloquial usage, the poet has remembered an earlier meaning of kind which is more appropriate to the context. As in 'human-kind' it denotes 'race', and thus, through the negative un-, we arrive at the meanings, 'beyond the world of men', 'against man', 'inhuman'. Here, the wind (*air*) is a natural force oblivious to the suffering of the people in the ship. So the word *unkind* has two functions. It is pulled by the homely *keeps* in the first (i.e. colloquial) direction and by infinite in the second. Our attention is engaged by this device, and we see the man/storm relationship in a new light.

Grammatical laws are brushed aside in the coining flint-flake. Two nouns have been combined to make a word which, because of its syntactical position, should have the function of an adjective (like black-backed, line 5), but which actually has the strength of a displaced noun (it is not 'flint-flaked') interpolated into the line against the rules of syntax. The poet wants us to visualize the flinty greyness of the sea and the white flakes of foam that it throws up, and to feel both the insubstantiality of water (soft, flaky) and its force (the toughness of flint); after unkind (in its usual sense), the idea of cruelty is also hinted at ('heart of flint'). Fint and flake must be grammatically welded into a compound because the two very different qualities of the sea are inseparable. Here, grammatical observance has been sacrificed in order to extend the descriptive range of the poem.

Wiry suggests, metaphorically, something sinewy and tough. This kind of personification has already been used in unkind, black-backed and sitting. Placed in the same line as whirlwind-swivelled, it may also help to establish a picture in which the spinning snow appears to the eye as coils of fine white wire. White-fiery conveys the fury of the snowstorm, destructive like fire and also, perhaps, burning the skin of the sailors exposed to it. A possible objection to this compound is that it grates on the ear: the first syllable of fiery is linked by assonance to wiry and almost linked to white. But the near similarity of these two sounds may lead to distortion, the diphthong of fiery being reduced to the vowel sound of white. This manipulation of sound is apparently deliberate, and our reaction to it is a matter of taste. The poet's intention may be to suggest the monotonous regularity of the storm's 'attack' on the ship.

Another compound, whirlwind-swivelled, also aims at a balance between meaning and suggestion through sound. Meaning is conveyed with the maximum brevity. The line taken as a whole seems to draw our attention from the general aspect of the snowstorm to the detail of the flurry, finally located in this adjective. The vowels move in one direction from the long 'i', suggesting continuous, steady blasts of air, through the 'er' of whirl (already faintly suggested in fiery) to the short 'i' (wind-swiv-). The vowels of whirlwind-swivelled are more

constricted than those of *wiry* and *fiery*. The movements of the tongue
required for the articulation of *whirlwind-swivelled* also help to
suggest the speed of the action it describes.

Although the coinings, *unchilding*, *unfathering*, are short-cuts to
meaning, they actually impede the movement of the verse line in
which they appear. But this seems to be deliberate. Meaning gives us
the different categories of people who are going to be bereaved;
rhythm brings the stanza to a climax in a thick cluster of stresses:

   wídow-making únchílding únfáthering

and *deeps* gains additional solemnity from the weight of adjectival
qualification which it bears.

Even this brief examination of words in poetry is enough to show us
that there is no Language of Poetry in the sense that certain words are
fit for poetic use and others not. Poets are not the custodians of some
esoteric 'word-horde'. But they do take upon themselves the
guardianship of words in a much fuller sense. A good poet often
seems to be taking words out of our mouths and using them more
effectively than we might have done.

When we attempt to write poetry, we are at once potential
conservers and explorers. Where Pope rescues his slang word from
oblivion by reminding us of its metaphorical content, Keats invents
compounds (*droop-headed*, *sand-wave*) to make his pictures more exact;
and Hopkins enriches his poetry with coinings like *flint-flake* and
unfathering. The aim they share is to revitalize language when it seems
in danger of going to sleep. The intellectual climate of their times
may decide the limits of this operation and, for the public reasons of
social history, as well as the private ones of experience and talent,
poets like Milton or Hopkins or Eliot may have been prepared to
allow themselves more liberties than Pope in stretching language
when the particular shadings of their own sensibilities can be
expressed in no other way. One of the legitimate functions of poetry
is to surprise us into attention and show us our apparently familiar
language in an unfamiliar dress.

THE VOICE

'Analytical' isn't invariably used as a term of endearment. The poet
whom Shakespeare imagined, his eye 'in a fine frenzy rolling', might

well have resented the suggestion that his poems could have been taken slowly apart and examined word by word; and he is entitled to a certain amount of sympathy: the critic who doesn't begin with a due sense of wonder that anything at all has been created out of 'airy nothing' may well be accused of a very arid form of intellectual pride. But the fact remains that analysis is one of the roads to the full appreciation of literature; and any of us who have faced the challenge of a sheet of blank paper know the difference between friendly enthusiasm and the possibly drier, but usually more memorable, comments of the reader who has paid us the compliment of setting out to discover what we were trying to do, and how near we came to doing it.

At its best, literary appreciation is a means towards getting to know a writer better. We sense the excitement which prompted Emily Dickinson to scribble 'Is this frostier?' at the bottom of a page after her sister-in-law had shown her that she had understood her intention in writing the poem. Any piece of writing has a voice: hence the critical term 'tone'. A poet recreating an experience through words and images and rhythms tries to communicate to us the mood which that experience originally generated and, if he is successful, we hear him speaking 'out of the page'. We may have sensed the still, recollected, rather bleak quality of Emily Dickinson's life from 'Safe in their Alabaster Chambers', or guessed at the pain for which Pope was trying to find an anodyne in his savage allusion to 'Sappho'. One cannot read either without being struck by their 'tone'.

But we should be on guard against the idea that tone in literature is necessarily the automatic, unconscious element it is in speech. For Wordsworth, poetry was 'emotion recollected in tranquillity': an angry poem is not necessarily the spontaneous effusion of an angry man; a sad poem, the work of someone paralysed by despair. Poetry is the recreation of experience, not a bathtub overflow of it; and tone, whilst ideally reflecting that experience, may be the result of the same degree of choice as, say, the decision to develop or suppress a certain metaphor.

In dramatic poetry, the writer has to create the tone appropriate to the speaker and the situation. An analysis of the following speeches from Act III of *Measure for Measure* will enable us to observe the means employed by Shakespeare for distinguishing between two differing temperaments and situations.

The setting is the condemned cell. In the first speech, the benevolent Duke of Vienna, who has the power to save the condemned man
(and has probably already made up his mind that Claudio will not be
executed for his crime of adultery), visits him disguised as a friar and,
in this assumed character, preaches a sermon on readiness for death.

> Thy best of rest is sleep,
> And that thou oft provok'st, yet grossly fear'st
> Thy death, which is no more. Thou art not thyself,
> For thou exists on many a thousand grains
> That issue out of dust. Happy thou art not,
> For what thou hast not, still thou striv'st to get,
> And what thou hast forget'st. Thou art not certain,
> For thy complexion shifts to strange affects,
> After the moon. If thou art rich, thou'rt poor,
> For like an ass whose back with ingots bows,
> Thou bear'st thy heavy riches but a journey,
> And death unloads thee.

The well-worn homiletic equations in these lines—death:
sleep; the body : dust; life : a journey—seem to belong to a
routine sermon, a consolation from a man who trades in comforts
which he has not examined too closely. It is in the structure, the
figures of speech and the diction that we actually *hear* the note of
shallow complacency in which the Duke imitates a Polonius among
friars.

Five sentences in succession have similar structures: a brief main
clause followed (in all but the first) by a subordinate adverbial
clause of reason introduced by *for*. The parallel structures are more
noticeable for being equal in length—they might be self-contained
couplets transposed into blank verse. We inevitably hear the voice
of a preacher who has mastered *some* of the laws of Rhetoric, reaching
the built-in pauses, rising to stresses, falling at stops at regular
intervals, with such contrived variations as the inversion of the
usual *thou art* structure in line 5 (*Happy thou art*) and the extended
length of the last sentence.

The impression of something contrived and mannered is given
also by such devices as the antithesis, wished-for sleep: feared death,
in lines 1–3; in the paradoxes, *Thou art not thyself* (*line 3*) and *If thou*

art rich, thou'rt poor (line 9), which score debating points, but on a note which is inappropriate to Claudio's situation; and in the pun, striv'st to get/forget'st (lines 6–7), which suggests a mind too conscious of its own ingenuity to be capable of associating itself with Claudio's suffering.

The mind reflected by the diction is world-weary. The Duke–Friar sees the world as either distasteful (grossly—line 2; dust—line 5) or trivial (shifts—line 8; ass—line 10; unloads—line 12). There is a high proportion of monosyllabic words in his speech—we hear the voice of a preacher who 'talks down' to ensure that he will be understood.

The second example is a speech made by Claudio, who believes that he is to die in a few hours. Like the Duke's speech, Claudio's borrows from the learning of the middle ages. Where the Duke's ideas and rhetorical manner were taken from homilies, Claudio's imagery comes from the medieval idea of the universe (later to be reproduced in Milton's Paradise Lost). The Earth is suspended from Heaven by a chain (pendent world—line 9); far below is Hell with its alternate torments of fiery floods (line 5) and thick-ribbed ice (line 6). But where the Duke's ideas are deliberately made to appear second-hand, Claudio's imagery is presented freshly to create the impression of l'homme moyen sensuel in agony at the expectancy of the Hell portrayed by medieval poets and theologians.

Ay, but to die, and go we know not where;
To lie in cold obstruction, and to rot;
This sensible warm motion to become
A kneaded clod; and the delighted spirit
To bathe in fiery floods, or to reside   5
In thrilling region of thick-ribbed ice;
To be imprisoned in the viewless winds
And blown with restless violence round about
The pendent world; or to be worse than worst
Of those that lawless and incertain thought   10
Imagine howling—'tis too horrible.
The weariest and most loathed worldly life
That age, ache, penury, and imprisonment
Can lay on nature, is a paradise
To what we fear of death.   15

The anguish reflected in this speech is chiefly concentrated round appeals to the sense of touch. *Sensible* (line 3)—'capable of feeling'—is the key-word. Claudio imagines the earth piled on his body (*cold obstruction*—line 2); and his once *warm* body actually being *kneaded* (line 4) like potter's clay. His idea of Hell is one of physical sensation: *bathing* in flame (line 5); feeling the sharp thrill of the imprisoning *ice* (line 6); of being blown about in a storm (lines 6–8). Significantly, his view of the living world includes *ache* (line 13). In contrast to the uncomfortable immediacy of what is felt, is the universal image of *The pendent world* (line 9), which with its new perspective virtually obliterates Claudio, reducing him to an atom; and the removal of all sign-posts in *viewless* (line 6) and *lawless and incertain thought* (line 10)—*lawless*—'not guided by scientific laws'. The man who apprehends the physical world through his senses is bewildered and lost when he contemplates an existence which can only be imagined in abstract terms.

The rhetoric of this speech is not the formal, limited scholastic rhetoric exemplified by the Duke's, but the poetic rhetoric which the dramatist uses to explore his character's situation and feelings in order to project them and stimulate corresponding feeling in the audience. A series of infinitives—*to die, to bathe, to reside, etc.*—becomes the collective subject of the verb *is* in line 11. Although the rules of syntax are satisfied by this device, the impression we receive as we hear or read the speech is of a cascade of ideas and images thundering into Claudio's mind and upsetting its balance so that, instead of formulated thoughts (subject and predicate), we have only a series of vividly conceived subjects, which—partly because of the urgency of the situation, and partly because of their individual and collective force—successfully defy the normal requirements of order, clarity and logic. The effect of this structure on tone is to create the impression of confused and anguished thinking aloud. Tension is built up by the delaying of the resolution, *'tis too horrible* (line 11), by the multiplication of phrases introduced by *and* or *or*; and the climax corresponds with Claudio's terrified realization that he doesn't know what to expect (lines 9–11). The brevity of the resolution in itself suggests the intensity of Claudio's anguish, since the one emotive adjective *horrible* is balanced against the weight of evidence he has produced to justify his emotion.

Anguish and confusion are also suggested by the variety of the diction, which veers from the monosyllabic simplicity of

> Ay, but to die, and go we know not where

to the half-abstract, latinate *cold obstruction* (where *obstruction* conveys through sound the idea of a body struggling against the weight of earth); the abstract *motion* (already softened by *warm*) is followed by the brutally material *kneaded clod*; the elusive, *delighted spirit* by bathe in *fiery floods*; the vivid *thick-ribbed ice* is governed by a formal, latinate verb, *reside*; the uncertainty of *viewless* (both 'unseeing' and 'unseen') and *restless violence* (again an abstract concept—the violence is not experienced as it was in the more concrete *kneaded clod* or *thick-ribbed ice*) is contrasted with the certainty of what is done to the victim—he is *imprison'd, blown about*—and with the pseudo-scientific fact of *The pendent world*. So the hopeless floundering of the sense-bound man as he speculates about the metaphysical world is reflected in a similar confusion of abstract and concrete terms. Again, the irrational hyperbole, *worst than worse*, adds to the feeling that we have entered a region of speculation where the usual guide-posts (in this case, grammar, reflecting logic) are no longer of use.

A comparative study of these speeches shows us that the dramatist has made his personages *sound* different, not just by giving them different ideas to express, but by making them express these ideas in quite different voices. The lopsided structure of Claudio's speech suggests extreme excitement; in the predictable balance of the Duke's we hear the prosing of an old man. Independently of their spoken thoughts, the Duke and Claudio have been made to betray, respectively, ascetic and sensual temperaments in words like *grossly* and *dust* (the Duke) and *warm, delighted, thrilling* (Claudio). The complacency of the Duke has been suggested by the use of a pun; the terrified confusion of Claudio by the oscillation between abstract words of Latin stock and Anglo-Saxon words that convey the realities of sensory experience.

W. H. Auden's treatment of a time-honoured theme has a deceptive simplicity. It is a sophisticated and witty exploration of words, phrases and grammatical forms which we usually take for granted. The verb *to be* is used in two senses—denoting Time (the difference between *This is, This was,* and *This will be*); and the state of Being (what *exists* and what *does not exist:* what is *real* and what is *not real*).

HIS EXCELLENCY

As it is, plenty;
As it's admitted
The children happy
And the car, the car
That goes so far,   5
And the wife devoted:
To this as it is,
To the work and the banks
Let his thinning hair
And his hauteur   10
Give thanks, give thanks.

All that was thought
As like as not is not;
When nothing was enough
But love, but love,   15
And the rough future
Of an intransigent nature,

And the betraying smile,
Betraying, but a smile:
That that is not, is not;   20
Forget, forget.

Let him not cease to praise,
Then, his lordly days;
Yes, and the success
Let him bless, let him bless: 25
Let him see in this
The profit larger
And the sin venial,
Lest he see as it is
The loss as major   30
And final, final.

W. H. AUDEN

1   Give a brief account of the theme.

2   'The poet goes out of his way to create an impression of naivety.' Do you agree?—If so, can you suggest why he should have done this?

3   Repetition is consciously used as a device to achieve more than one effect. What effects?

4   Attempt a paraphrase of lines 18–19.

5   Consider the interplay between meaning and verbal mood and tense.

6   Consider the tone of the third stanza. In what circumstances would the subjunctive 'Let . . .' form usually be found? Is the cross-reference deliberate?

7   How many interpretations of the phrase *as it is* are implied?

8   'All head and no heart' or 'A moving account of the human condition': which do you think is nearer the truth?

TWO

Rupert Brooke and Wilfred Owen produced their best work while on
active service during the First World War. Both the following poems
are elegiac, and they contain closely related images; but they reveal
widely different states of mind—states to which the respective verse
forms seem ideally suited.

A

THE DEAD

These hearts were woven of human joys and cares,
  Washed marvellously with sorrow, swift to mirth.
The years had given them kindness. Dawn was theirs,
  And sunset, and the colours of the earth.
These had seen movement, and heard music; known   5
  Slumber and waking; loved; gone proudly friended;
Felt the quick stir of wonder; sat alone;
  Touched flowers and furs and cheeks. All this is ended.

There are waters blown by changing winds to laughter
And lit by the rich skies, all day. And after,   10
  Frost, with a gesture, stays the waves that dance
And wandering loveliness. He leaves a white
  Unbroken glory, a gathered radiance,
A width, a shining peace, under the night.

RUPERT BROOKE

1   Has the poet succeeded in conveying as a poetic experience (or experiences) the sense of living intensely and enjoyably?

2   Consider the relationship in this sonnet between octave and sestet.

3   Examine the interplay of changing verb tenses. Is the meaning of the poem affected by the changes?

4   Has the poet mastered the sonnet form or has the sonnet mastered him?

5   Analyse the imagery of the sestet. Try to distinguish between its appeals to visual memory, feeling and intellect.

6   Examine the syntax of the poem. Does it help to reproduce a poetic experience?

B

FUTILITY

Move him into the sun—
Gently its touch awoke him once,
At home, whispering of fields unsown.
Always it woke him, even in France,
Until this morning and this snow.   5
If anything might rouse him now
The kind old sun will know.

Think how it wakes the seeds—
Woke, once, the clays of a cold star.
Are limbs, so dear-achieved, are sides,   10
Full-nerved—still warm—too hard to stir?
Was it for this the clay grew tall?
—O what made fatuous sunbeams toil
To break earth's sleep at all?

WILFRED OWEN

1   Do you find anything inherent in the theme of the poem that
insists on the two stanza form?

2   Examine the ways by which a sudden change of mood is
induced.

3   'The poetic experience is identified with a single image.' Do you
agree?

4   'The poem is weakened by its anthropomorphic view of life.'
Is this a fair judgment?

5   Are the movement and sound of this verse compatible with its
title?

6   Consider the use of the following words:
     once (lines 2 and 9), day (lines 9 and 12), this (lines 5 and 12)

COMPARATIVE STUDY

1   The years had given them kindness (A)

     . . . whispering of fields unsown (B)

     Consider the degrees of success with which the two poets have
conveyed the experience of waste and lost opportunity.

2   Would it be reasonable to distinguish between the two as
between rawness and technical accomplishment?

3   Which do you prefer?

THREE

Gerard Manley Hopkins takes one of the great themes of poetry and renders it down to its bare bones. If this poem succeeds, it does so through its brevity and its swift, inevitable progression from one bald statement to another, until we come back to the first term of the argument as if completing a circle. It is sparse but its appeals to our feelings are deftly aimed. The ambiguous title and the note 'to a young child'—more a stage direction than a dedication—are important to a lyric which depends for its effectiveness on quickly establishing a dramatic situation. Hopkins is using sprung rhythm (in which there is no attempt to make a regular distribution of stresses as in conventional metres) and the lines have between two (line 1) and four (line 8) stressed syllables.

SPRING AND FALL
(to a young child)

Margaret, are you grieving
Over Goldengrove unleaving?
Leaves, like the things of man, you
With your fresh thoughts care for, can you?
Ah! as the heart grows older   5
It will come to such sights colder
By and by, nor spare a sigh
Though worlds of wanwood leafmeal lie;
And yet you will weep and know why.
Now no matter, child, the name: 10
Sorrow's springs are the same.

Nor mouth had, no nor mind, expressed
What heart heard of, ghost guessed:
It is the blight man was born for,
It is Margaret you mourn for.   15

GERARD MANLEY HOPKINS

1   Describe the situation that the poet envisages.

2   How does Margaret's immediate response differ from her
imagined future reactions to autumn?

3   Describe the poet's a) immediate and b) recollected responses
to Margaret's behaviour.

4   Attempt a statement of the theme in your own words.

5   Consider the following words in their contexts:

   Goldengrove (line 2), wanwood (line 7), leafmeal (line 8),
   springs (line 11), blight (line 14).
Can the coinings be justified?

6   'The rhymes and rhythm combine to form a jingle quite
innappropriate to the mood suggested by the subject.' Could you
refute this opinion?

7   Consider the effect of the 'feminine' rhymes in the first three,
and the final, couplets.

8   To what extent has the structure of the poem been influenced
by a) the imagery, and b) the verse form?

9   Paraphrase lines 12 and 13. (Pay special attention to the
metaphors and the archaic use of 'ghost'.) Can the obscurity of this
couplet be justified?

FOUR

A

ON THE MOVE
'Man, you gotta Go'

The blue jay scuffling in the bushes follows
Some hidden purpose, and the gust of birds
That spurts across the field, the wheeling swallows,
Have nested in the trees and undergrowth.
Seeking their instinct, or their poise, or both,   5
One moves with an uncertain violence
Under the dust thrown by a baffled sense
Or the dull thunder of approximate words.

On motorcycles, up the road, they come:
Small, black, as flies hanging in heat, the Boys,   10
Until the distance throws them forth, their hum
Bulges to thunder held by calf and thigh.
In goggles, donned impersonality,
In gleaming jackets trophied with the dust,
They strap in doubt—by hiding it, robust—   15
And almost hear a meaning in their noise.

Exact conclusion of their hardiness
Has no shape yet, but from known whereabouts
They ride, direction where the tires press.
They scare a flight of birds across the field: 20
Much that is natural, to the will must yield.
Men manufacture both machine and soul,
And use what they imperfectly control
To dare a future from the taken routes.

It is a part solution, after all.   25
One is not necessarily discord
On earth; or damned because, half animal,
One lacks direct instinct, because one wakes
Afloat on movement that divides and breaks.
One joins the movement in a valueless world,   30
Choosing it, till, both hurler and the hurled,
One moves as well, always toward, toward.

A minute holds them, who have come to go:
The self-defined, astride the created will
They burst away; the towns they travel through   35
Are home for neither bird nor holiness,
For birds and saints complete their purposes.
At worst, one is in motion; and at best,
Reaching no absolute, in which to rest,
One is always nearer by not keeping still.   40

THOM GUNN

1   What view of human life does this poem attempt to convey?

2   Some hidden purpose (line 2)
         One lacks direct instinct (line 28)

    Explore the contrast drawn between animals following their
instincts and man grappling with the responsibility of free will.

3   direction where the tires press (line 19)
         astride the created will (line 34)

    Consider the contrast between the apparent aimlessness of the
Boys' behaviour, and the unconscious recognition of the nature of
life which the poet believes it to reflect.

4   Consider the importance of the following metaphors and
similes in helping to bridge the gap between the material and
metaphysical aspects of the events described:

         as flies hanging in heat (line 10)

> They strap in doubt (line 15)
> Men manufacture both machine and soul (line 22)

5   What is the significance of the grammatical incompleteness of
       always toward, toward (line 32)
     and   One is always nearer (line 40)?
     Which line in the last stanza illuminates these phrases?

6   What is the effect of
       A minute holds them, who have come to go (line 33)?

B

ESSENTIAL BEAUTY

In frames as large as rooms that face all ways
And block the ends of streets with giant loaves,
Screen graves with custard, cover slums with praise
Of motor-oil and cuts of salmon, shine
Perpetually these sharply-pictured groves   5
Of how life should be. High above the gutter
A silver knife sinks into golden butter,
A glass of milk stands in a meadow, and
Well-balanced families, in fine
Midsummer weather, owe their smiles, their cars,   10
Even their youth, to that small cube each hand
Stretches towards. These, and the deep armchairs
Aligned to cups at bedtime, radiant bars
(Gas or electric), quarter-profile cats
By slippers on warm mats,   15
Reflect none of the rained-on streets and squares

They dominate outdoors. Rather, they rise
Serenely to proclaim pure crust, pure foam,

Pure coldness to our live imperfect eyes
That stare beyond this world, where nothing's made   20
As new or washed quite clean, seeking the home
All such inhabit. There, dark raftered pubs
Are filled with white-clothed ones from tennis-clubs,
And the boy puking his heart out in the Gents
Just missed them as the pensioner paid   25
A halfpenny more for Granny Graveclothes' Tea
To taste old age, and dying smokers sense
Walking towards them through some dappled park
As if on water that unfocused she
No match lit up, nor drag ever brought near,   30
Who now stands newly clear,
Smiling and recognizing, and going dark.

PHILIP LARKIN

1   What aspects of the techniques and psychology of advertising
is the poet interested in?

2   Is the title appropriate? Consider the relationship between it
and the repeated 'pure' (lines 18–19).

3   Explore the significance of

          cover slums with praise
     Of motor-oil and cuts of salmon

     and   the pensioner paid
          A halfpenny more for Granny Graveclothes' Tea
          To taste old age . . .

4   What attitude to life is revealed by the varying register of the
diction in the second part?

     e.g. serenely, pure, white-clothed, dappled:
          puking, Graveclothes, drag.

5   Consider the element of humour. What qualifying adjective
would you apply to it if you were discussing the tone of this writing?

6   Is there any link between the poet's intention and the use of
rhyme?

7   Consider the approach to language reflected in the following (considered in their contexts):

well-balanced (line 9), radiant (line 13), drag (line 30).

COMPARATIVE STUDY

1   Both poets see human life in terms of a quest. Compare the ways in which they have embodied this idea in their poems.

2   Are these reflections of contemporary life equally dispassionate?

3   Make a comparative study of the two poems, paying special attention to a) descriptive power, and b) insight.

4   'The difference in tone between these poems could be considered as that between a dissatisfaction that lives in hope and a dissatisfaction which is convinced there is nothing better.' Discuss.

5   Which do you consider the more ambitious work? Have both poets succeeded in doing what they set out to do?

FIVE

John Keats and D. H. Lawrence have chosen similar starting points in conveying their feelings about the nature of life. They are both concerned with buried civilizations, Keats with the Ancient Greek, Lawrence with the Etruscan; and each offers for consideration the object which has given him his imaginative experience of the past. Each poem is in the form of a reverie, and in each there is an attempt to establish the subject of the reverie (the Urn and the Cypresses) as a symbol.

A

ODE ON A GRECIAN URN

Thou still unravish'd bride of quietness,
Thou foster-child of silence and slow time,
Sylvan historian, who canst thus express
A flowery tale more sweetly than our rhyme:
What leaf-fring'd legend haunts about thy shape   5
Of deities or mortals, or of both,
In Tempe or the dales of Arcady?
What men or gods are these? What maidens loth?
What mad pursuit? What struggle to escape?
What pipes and timbrels? What wild ecstacy?   10

Heard melodies are sweet, but those unheard
Are sweeter; therefore, ye soft pipes, play on;
Not to the sensual ear, but more endear'd
Pipe to the spirit ditties of no tone:

Fair youth, beneath the trees, thou canst not leave   15
Thy song, nor ever can those trees be bare;
Bold lover, never, never canst thou kiss,
Though winning near the goal—yet, do not grieve;
She cannot fade, though thou hast not thy bliss,
For ever wilt thou love. and she be fair!   20

Ah, happy, happy boughs! that cannot shed
Your leaves, nor ever bid the Spring adieu;
And, happy melodist, unwearied,
For ever piping songs for ever new;
More happy love! more happy, happy love!   25
For ever warm and still to be enjoy'd,
For ever panting, and for ever young;
All breathing human passion far above,
That leaves a heart high-sorrowful and cloy'd,
A burning forehead, and a parching tongue.   30

Who are these coming to the sacrifice?
To what green altar, O mysterious priest,
Lead'st thou that heifer lowing at the skies,
And all her silken flanks with garlands drest?
What little town by river or sea shore,   35
Or mountain-built with peaceful citadel,
Is emptied of its folk, this pious morn?
And, little town, thy streets for evermore
Will silent be: and not a soul to tell
Why thou art desolate, can e'er return.   40

O Attic shape! Fair attitude! with brede
Of marble men and maidens overwrought,
With forest branches and the trodden weed;
Thou silent form dost tease us out of thought
As doth eternity: Cold Pastoral!   45
When old age shall this generation waste,
Thou shalt remain, in midst of other woe
Than ours, a friend to man, to whom thou say'st,
'Beauty is truth, truth beauty,'—that is all
Ye know on earth, and all ye need to know.   50

JOHN KEATS

1   'Silence', 'piping', 'saying'. Has this imagery any thematic significance?

2   Is there any truth in the suggestion that some of the stanza divisions mark changing attitudes towards the Urn?

3   In stanza 4 the poet appears to forget one of the qualities with which he endowed the Urn in stanza 1. Is there anything in the diction of stanza 5 to suggest that he later wants to re-emphasize that quality?

4   Paraphrase 'Pipe to the spirit ditties of no tone' (line 14).

5   Comment on the repetitions in stanza 3.

6   'An awareness of statements and questions balanced against each other is important to an understanding of this poem.' Do you agree?

7   Consider the relationship between form and content.

B

(The Etruscans, inhabitants of Etruria—which roughly corresponded to the modern Italian region of Tuscany—have been described as 'the most mysterious people of antiquity'. They are known chiefly from the works of art that archaeologists have recovered—including the enigmatically smiling figures which impressed Lawrence (line 14)— and from the probably falsified accounts of them given by their Roman conquerors. The reference in line 51 is to Leonardo da Vinci's painting, the 'Mona Lisa'. Montezuma, the Aztec King, died in the hands of the first Spanish invaders of Mexico.)

CYPRESSES

Tuscan cypresses,
What is it?

Folded in like a dark thought
For which the language is lost,
Tuscan cypresses,   5
Is there a great secret?
Are our words no good?

The undeliverable secret,
Dead with a dead race and a dead speech, and yet
Darkly monumental in you,   10
Etruscan cypresses.

Ah, how I admire your fidelity,
Dark cypresses!

Is it the secret of the long-nose Etruscans?
The long-nosed, sensitive-footed, subtly-smiling Etruscans,   15
Who made so little noise outside the cypress groves?

Among the sinuous, flame-tall cypresses
That swayed their length of darkness all around
Etruscan-dusky, wavering men of old Etruria:
Naked except for fanciful long shoes,   20
Going with insidious half-smiling quietness
And some of Africa's imperturbable sang-froid
About a forgotten business.

What business, then?
Nay tongues are dead, and words are hollow as hollow seed-   25
    pods,
Having shed their sound and finished all their echoing
Etruscan syllables,
That had the telling.

Yet more I see you darkly concentrate,
Tuscan cypresses,   30
On one old thought:
On one old slim imperishable thought, while you remain
Etruscan cypresses;
Dusky, slim marrow-thought of slender, flickering men of
    Etruria,   35
Whom Rome called vicious.

Vicious, dark cypresses:
Vicious, you supple, brooding, softly-swaying pillars of dark
    flame.
Monumental to a dead, dead race
Embowered in you!

Were they then vicious, the slender, tender-footed   40
Long-nosed men of Etruria?
Or was their way only evasive and different, dark like
    cypress-trees in a wind?

They are dead with all their vices,
And all that is left
Is the shadowy monomania of some cypresses   45
And tombs.

The smile, the subtle Etruscan smile still lurking
Within the tombs,
Etruscan cypresses.

He laughs longest who laughs last;   50
Nay, Leonardo only bungled the pure Etruscan smile.

What would I not give
To bring back the rare and orchid-like
Evil-yclept Etruscan?

For as to the evil   55
We have only Roman word for it,
Which I, being a little weary of Roman virtue,
Don't hang much weight on.

For oh, I know, in the dust where we have buried
The silenced races and all their abominations,   60
We have buried so much of the delicate magic of life.

There in the deeps
That churn the frankincense and ooze the myrrh,
Cypress shadowy,
Such an aroma of lost human life!   65

They say the fit survive,
But I invoke the spirits of the lost.
Those that have not survived, the darkly lost,
To bring their meaning back into life again,
Which they have taken away   70
And wrapt inviolable in soft cypress trees,
Etruscan cypresses.

Evil, what is evil?
There is only one evil, to deny life
As Rome denied Etruria   75
And mechanical America Montezuma still.

D. H. LAWRENCE

1   How does the poet resurrect the Etruscans a) historically and
b) imaginatively?

2   Has Lawrence convinced you that the following words and
simile can be applied to the cypress trees?

> like a dark thought
> For which the language is lost (lines 3–4)

> fidelity (line 12), darkly concentrate (line 29), vicious (line 36),
> monomania (line 45).

3   Do the following give you an experience of the Etruscans?
> wavering (line 19), flickering (line 34), like cypress trees in a
> wind (line 42).

4   The language of the Etruscans has been preserved on their
monuments but can no longer be deciphered. How has the poet
drawn our attention to this fact?

5   Are lines 51 and 76 distracting interpolations or an integral
part of the poem?

6   'Sensitive verse which lends itself to the illusion that the poetic
experience is simultaneous with the act of writing the poem.'

> 'A shapeless and repetitive piece of writing.'
> Which of these opinions do you consider to be nearer the truth?

7   Consider the use made of compound words, proverbs, truisms
and colloquialisms.

8   Is there a poetic experience here, or only a series of half-realized experiences?

COMPARATIVE STUDY

1   Both poets lead us through questioning, and in a deliberately established atmosphere of perplexity, to a final statement. Are these statements equally convincing in their contexts?

2   What does the Urn, and what do the Cypresses, symbolize? Have they been established with equal success as symbols?

3   'In both poems there is a tension between the desire to give feeling a memorable shape (and create a work of art) and the desire to involve the reader by giving the impression of thinking aloud.' Do you agree?—If so, have Keats and Lawrence been equally successful in maintaining that tension?

4   Has either of the poets lost or gained through his choice of a verse form?

SIX

Although Alexander Pope's 'Eloisa to Abelard' and George Crabbe's 'Peter Grimes' are clearly related stylistically, nearly a hundred years come between their publication dates; and Crabbe, using a verse form perfected by Pope and the Augustans, was writing in the age of Wordsworth. Consequently the poets' different approaches to the concept of Man and Nature must be seen in relation to a changing climate of sensibility.

A

(The dramatic monologue from which these lines are taken is based on the Eloisa and Abelard story. Pope imagines Eloisa, finally separated from her Abelard, and living in a convent, addressing these words to him in absence. A teacher of philosophy and a cleric, Abelard had made love to her while she was his pupil, and later married her.)

In these lone walls (their day's eternal bound)
These moss-grown domes with spiry turrets crown'd,
Where awful arches make a noon-day night,
And the dim windows shed a solemn light;
Thy eyes diffus'd a reconciling ray,   5
And gleams of glory brighten'd all the day.
But now no face divine contentment wears,
'Tis all blank sadness, or continual tears.
See how the force of others pray'rs I try,
(O pious fraud of am'rous charity!)   10
But why should I on others pray'rs depend?

Come thou, my father, brother, husband, friend!
Ah let thy handmaid, sister, daughter move,
And all those tender names in one, thy love!
The darksome pines that o'er yon rocks reclin'd,   15
Wave high, and murmur to the hollow wind,
The wand'ring streams that shine between the hills,
The grots that echo to the tinkling rills,
The dying gales that pant upon the trees,
The lakes that quiver to the curling breeze;   20
No more these scenes my meditation aid,
Or lull to rest the visionary maid.
But o'er the twilight groves and dusky caves,
Long-sounding aisles, and intermingled graves,
Black Melancholy sits, and round her throws   25
A death-like silence, and a dread repose:
Her gloomy presence saddens all the scene,
Shades ev'ry flow'r and darkens ev'ry green,
Deepens the murmur of the falling floods,
And breathes a browner horror on the woods.   30

ALEXANDER POPE

1   Consider the writer's intention in placing this descriptive
passage in a dramatic monologue.

2   Examine the way in which the idea of contrast is developed.
Explain its significance.

3   Consider the effectiveness of the oxymoron, 'noon-day night'
(line 3). Try to find other examples of this device in the passage.
Are they successful?

4   Consider the following words in their contexts. Do you think
they are well chosen?
      awful (line 3), shed (line 4), darksome (line 15), hollow (line 16),
      curling (line 20), twilight (line 23), floods (line 29).

5   Examine the use of personification in lines 19–30. To what
extent does it contribute to a) the poetic experience, and b) the unity
of the passage?

6   Analyse lines 15–16; 19; and 29–30. Pay special attention to
metrical and other sound effects.

B

(These lines are taken from a narrative poem, 'Peter Grimes'. Peter, a fisherman, has voluntarily exiled himself from an East Anglian fishing community after the spread of rumours concerning the deaths of two of his apprentices.)

Thus by himself compell'd to live each day,
To wait for certain hours the Tide's delay:
At the same times the same dull views to see,
The bounding Marsh-bank and the blighted Tree;
The Water only, when the Tides were high,   5
When low, the Mud half-cover'd and half-dry;
The Sun-burn'd Tar that blisters on the Planks,
And Bank-side Stakes in their uneven ranks;
Heaps of entangled Weeds that slowly float,
As the Tide rolls by the impeded Boat.   10
When Tides were neap, and, in the sultry day,
Through the tall bounding Mud-banks made their way,
Which on each side rose swelling, and below
The dark warm Flood ran silently and slow;
There anchoring, Peter chose from Man to hide,   15
There hang his Head, and view the lazy Tide
In its hot slimy Channel slowly glide;
Where the small Eels that left the deeper way
For the warm Shore, within the Shallows play;
Where gaping Muscles, left upon the Mud,   20
Slope their slow passage to the fallen Flood;—
Here dull and hopeless he'd lie down and trace
How side-long Crabs had scrawl'd their crooked race;
Or sadly listen to the tuneless cry
Of fishing Gull or clanging Golden-Eye;   25
What time the Sea-Birds to the marsh would come,
And the loud Bittern from the Bull-rush home,
Gave from the Salt-ditch side the bellowing Boom:
He nurst the Feelings these dull Scenes produce,
And lov'd to stop beside the opening Sluice;   30
Where the small Stream, confin'd in narrow bound,
Ran with a dull, unvaried, sad'ning sound;

Where all presented to the Eye or Ear,
Oppress'd the Soul with Misery, Grief and Fear.

GEORGE CRABBE

1   There anchoring, Peter chose from Man to hide (line 15)

       And lov'd to stop beside the opening Sluice (line 30)

       How has the writer blended this aspect of the situation with the
idea of bleakness, on which he relies to awaken the reader's sympathy
for Peter?

2   Has the poet succeeded in conveying the physical conditions of
Peter Grimes's daily life?

3   'Spoiled by repetitiveness.' Is this a valid judgment?

4   Try to distinguish between the parts played by a) subject
matter and b) metrical and other sound effects, in establishing the
mood of the first ten lines.

5   Consider the following words in their contexts. Do you think
they are well chosen?

       lazy (line 16), Slope (line 22), side-long (line 23), scrawl'd (line
       23), clanging (line 25), bellowing (line 28).

COMPARATIVE STUDY

1   Which poet has been the more successful in placing his subject
in a setting?

2   'Pope, making a rare excursion beyond the formal garden, has
a cosier view of Nature and man's relationship to it than Crabbe.'
Is this fair?

3   On the showing of these extracts, which poet has the greater
understanding of human experience?

4   Pope and Crabbe are trying to create pathos (i.e. to make us feel
sorry for Eloisa and Peter). Consider the different means they have
used, and the degrees of success they have had in achieving this aim.

SEVEN

Gerard Manley Hopkins ('Carrion Comfort') was a great admirer of the poetry of George Herbert ('Affliction'). The poet of the nineteenth century and the poet of the early seventeenth have much in common apart from their poetic achievement. Both were ministers of religion; both subordinated considerable literary gifts to the demands of religious asceticism. In poems like those that follow, the poetic experience they have attempted to reproduce is of a tension between the demands of the ascetic impulse and those of the senses and of ambition. Neither poet received recognition during his lifetime.

A

(After a brilliant early career at Cambridge, George Herbert gave up the chance of worldly advancement and became the rector of a small country parish.)

AFFLICTION

When first thou didst entice to thee my heart,
   I thought the service brave:
So many joys I writ down for my part,
   Besides what I might have
Out of my stock of naturall delights,
Augmented with thy gracious benefits.

I looked on thy furniture so fine,
   And made it fine to me,

5

Thy glorious household-stuffe did me entwine,
   And 'tice me unto thee.   10
Such stores I counted mine: both heav'n and earth
Payd me my wages in a world of mirth.

What pleasures could I want whose King I served,
   Where joyes my fellows were?
Thus argu'd into hopes, my thoughts reserved   15
   No place for grief or fear;
Therefore my sudden soul caught at the place,
And made her youth and fierceness seek thy face.

At first thou gav'st me milk and sweetnesses
   I had my wish and way: 20
My days were straw'd with flow'rs and happinesse;
   There was no month but May.
But with my yeares sorrow did twist and grow,
And made a party unawares for wo.

My flesh began unto my soul in pain,   25
   'Sicknesses cleave my bones,
Consuming agues dwell in ev'ry vein,
   And tune my breath to grones':
Sorrow was all my soul; I scarce beleeved,
Till grief did tell me roundly, that I lived.   30

When I got health, thou took'st away my life,
   And more; for my friends die:
My mirth and edge was lost; a blunted knife
   Was of more use than I.
Thus thinne and lean without a fence or friend,   35
I was blown through with ev'ry storm and winde.

Whereas my birth and spirit rather took
   The way that takes the town;
Thou didst betray me to a lingring book
   And wrap me in a gown.   40
I was entangled in the world of strife,
Before I had the power to change my life.

Yet, for I threatned oft the siege to raise,
  Not simpering all mine age,
Thou often didst with academick praise   45
  Melt and dissolve my rage.
I took the sweetned pill, till I came neare;
I could not go away, nor persevere.

Yet lest perchance I should too happie be
  In my unhappinesse,   50
Turning my purge to food, thou throwest me
  Into more sicknesses.
Thus dost thy power cross-bias me, not making
Thine own gift good, yet me from my ways taking.

Now I am here, what wilt thou do with me   55
  None of my books will show:
I read, and sigh, and wish I were a tree;
  For sure then I should grow
To fruit or shade: at least some bird would trust
Her household to me, and I should be just.   60

Yet, though thou troublest me, I must be meek;
  In weaknesse must be stout.
Well, I will change the service, and go seek
  Some other master out.
Ah my deare God! though I am clean forgot,   65
Let me not love thee, if I love thee not.

GEORGE HERBERT

1   'The bare bones of personal experience obtrude through the
allegory.' Is this a blemish?

2   'A religious experience awkwardly described in terms of petty
commerce and court life.' Discuss this view of the poem.

3   Examine the paradoxes in stanzas 9 and 11. Can their obscurity
be justified?

4   '. . . I threatned oft the siege to raise' (stanza 8) seems to bring
a new element into the poem. How would you interpret the
metaphor? Does it anticipate any future development?

5   Analyse the poetic effect of stanza 10.

6   Consider the choice of verse-form and the use made of it.

B

CARRION COMFORT

Not, I'll not, carrion comfort, Despair, not feast on thee;
Not untwist—slack they may be—these last strands of man
In me or, most weary, cry I can no more, I can;
Can something, hope, wish day come, not choose not to be.
But ah, but O thou terrible, why wouldst thou rude on me   5
Thy wring-world right foot rock? lay a lion limb against
    me? scan
With darksome devouring eyes my bruised bones? and fan,
O in turns of tempest, me heaped there, me frantic to avoid
    thee and flee?
Why? That my chaff might fly; my grain lie, sheer and clear.
Nay in all that toil, that coil, since (seems) I kissed the rod,   10
Hand rather, my heart lo! lapped strength, stole joy, would
    laugh, cheer.
Cheer whom though? the hero whose heaven-handling flung
    me, foot trod
Me? or me that fought him? O which one? is it each one?
    That night, that year
Of now done darkness I wretch lay wrestling with (My
    God!) my God.

GERARD MANLEY HOPKINS

1   What is the dominant image in this poem?

2   Discuss the imagery of the first line. What attitude towards
despair does it imply?

3   Is the tortuous nature of this poem accidental or deliberate? If the latter, how has the effect been produced, and for what reason?

4   One word in line 7 provides a link between the poem's controlling image and a new metaphor. Examine the new image, and try to decide if it is appropriate to this context.

5   In the absence of conventional metre, what part do a) meaning and b) sound play in determining the rhythm of this verse?

6   What attitude towards himself does the poet's choice of metaphors in line 11 suggest?

7   Consider the choice of verse form and the use made of it.

COMPARATIVE STUDY

1   What have the two poets in common in their approach to religious poetry?

2   Both poets recognize an ambivalence in their attitude towards religion. Have they succeeded in presenting this fact objectively?

3   Have the poets gained or lost through their choice of verse forms?

4   What poetic virtues do George Herbert and Gerard Manley Hopkins share?

EIGHT

A

HE BIDS HIS BELOVED BE AT PEACE

I hear the Shadowy Horses, their long manes a-shake,
Their hoofs heavy with tumult, their eyes glimmering white;
The North unfolds above them clinging, creeping night,
The East her hidden joy before the morning break,
The West weeps in pale dew and sighs passing away,   5
The South is pouring down roses of crimson fire:
O vanity of Sleep, Hope, Dream, endless Desire,
The Horses of Disaster plunge in the heavy clay:
Beloved, let your eyes half close, and your heart beat
Over my heart, and your hair fall over my breast,   10
Drowning love's lonely hour in deep twilight of rest,
And hiding their tossing manes and their tumultuous feet.

W. B. YEATS

1   Has W. B. Yeats succeeded in establishing symbolically the
states-of-being listed in line 7? What relevance have these states to
the situation imagined in the last four lines?

2   Consider the effect of the 'Shadowy Horses' symbol and, in
particular:

> Their hoofs heavy with tumult . . . (line 2)
> and   . . . plunge in the heavy clay (line 8).

3   Analyse the diction of lines 3–6, relating it to the experience the
poet is trying to reproduce.

4   Examine the interplay of rhythm and sense in lines 7–10.

5   Attempt an analysis of the poetic effect of line 11.

B

SICK LOVE

O Love, be fed with apples while you may,
And feel the sun and go in royal array,
A smiling innocent on the heavenly causeway,

Though in what listening horror for the cry
That soars in outer blackness dismally,   5
The dumb blind beast, the paranoiac fury:

Be warm, enjoy the season, lift your head,
Exquisite in the pulse of tainted blood,
That shivering glory not to be despised,

Take your delight in momentariness,   10
Walk between dark and dark—a shining space
With the grave's narrowness, though not its peace.

ROBERT GRAVES

1   What aspect of love does Robert Graves wish to emphasize?

2   What does the causeway (line 3) symbolize? Examine the
development of the symbol throughout the poem.

3   What is 'The dumb blind beast, the paranoiac fury'?

4   How are we reminded of stanza 2 in the affirmations of stanzas
3 and 4?

5   Explain the use of 'what' in line 4 and consider the effect of its
use on the tone of the stanza.

6   What contribution does the imagery of line 12 make towards
the total effect of the poem?

COMPARATIVE STUDY

1   Yeats and Graves seem very close here in their experience of
life. By examining the structure of their poems and their use of

imagery, would it be possible to demonstrate that they are also close in technique?

2   Consider the function of imagery in these poems.

3   Among Robert Graves's essays, there is a satirical attack on a poem by Yeats. After examining these poems, would it be possible to suggest what aspects of Yeats's writing Graves disliked? Do you think he was pointing at a literary weakness, or merely voicing an antipathy for a writer with a different temperament?

NINE

Passage A is taken from 'An Epistle to Dr Arbuthnot', the satirical poem
in which Pope reviews his own career and the literary climate of the
early eighteenth century. B is a poem by R. S. Thomas. Both Pope and
Thomas seem to have felt the need to make up their minds about
people whose attitudes they distrust, and the modern poet, though
his attitude towards Cynddylan is far less hostile than Pope's to
Bufo, has recalled some of the devices and mannerisms that
characterize the Augustan satirical portrait.

A

(Bufo, to whom a new edition of Horace seems to have been
dedicated, considers himself a patron of the arts, and is therefore
associated with Apollo, the god of music. His library is adorned with
classical statues and busts, some of them labelled with more
enthusiasm than accuracy.)

Proud as Apollo on his forked hill,
Sat full-blown Bufo, puff'd by ev'ry quill;
Fed with soft Dedication all day long,
Horace and he went hand in hand in song.
His Library (where busts of Poets dead   5
And a true Pindar stood without a head)
Receiv'd of wits an undistinguish'd race,
Who first his judgment ask'd, and then a place:
Much they extoll'd his pictures, much his seat,
And flatter'd ev'ry day, and some days eat: 10

Till grown more frugal in his riper days,
He paid some bards with port, and some with praise,
To some a dry rehearsal was assign'd,
And others (harder still) he paid in kind.
Dryden alone (what wonder?) came not nigh,   15
Dryden alone escap'd this judging eye:
But still the Great have kindness in reserve,
He help'd to bury whom he help'd to starve.

ALEXANDER POPE

1   What faculty is missing from Bufo's personality?

2   Suggest an interpretation of line 4.

3   'The sudden transition from the general to the particular at the
end of the passage weakens it considerably.' Do you agree?

4   Try to unravel the various strands of wit, jocularity and heavy
irony in this passage. What shifts of attitude are revealed by these
changes of tone?

5   Examine the structure of lines 8–10, considering the relationship between style and intention.

6   What effect do the parentheses in lines 14 and 15 have on the
tone?

7   Consider the interplay of sound and sense in lines 1–4. Can
you find other examples of such interplay?

8   Has language been used poetically in this passage?

B

CYNDDYLAN ON A TRACTOR

Ah, you should see Cynddylan on a tractor.
Gone the old look that yoked him to the soil;
He's a new man now, part of the machine,
His nerves of metal and his blood oil.

The clutch curses, but the gears obey   5
His least bidding, and lo, he's away
Out of the farmyard, scattering hens.
Riding to work now as a great man should,
He is the knight at arms breaking the fields'
Mirror of silence, emptying the wood   10
Of foxes and squirrels and bright jays.
The sun comes over the tall trees
Kindling all the hedges, but not for him
Who runs his engine on a different fuel.
And all the birds are singing, bills wide in vain,   15
As Cynddylan passes proudly up the lane.

R. S. THOMAS

1   What diminishment does Cynddylan undergo on a tractor?

2   What is the poet's attitude to a) Cynddylan and b) Nature? How
are these attitudes revealed in his style?

3   Examine line 4, and consider its effect on the immediate
development of the poem.

4   Suggest an interpretation of lines 9–11. Is the image a) accurate
and b) appropriate?

5   Is the use of anticlimax deliberate or accidental?

6   Analyse the poetic effect of the concluding couplet.

7   Try to justify the inversion in line 2, and the use of the following words:

    ah (line 1), curses (line 5), great (line 8), bright (line 11), tall
    (line 12), and (line 15).

COMPARATIVE STUDY

1   Both poets describe threats to their particular worlds; but both
choose to play down any anxiety they may feel. Why? And how?

2   In order to convince us of the truth of their judgments, Pope
and R. S. Thomas have to get us on their side. How do they do this?

3   Would it be true to say that 'Cynddylan on a Tractor', unlike the extract from 'An Epistle to Dr Arbuthnot', has a built-in unity and completeness?—If so, what stylistic feature helps to give it these qualities?

4   Consider the interplay in each poem between tone and the choice of images or allusions.

TEN

Consider the views on the function and content of poetry conveyed in the following poems by Robert Graves.

THE COOL WEB

Children are dumb to say how hot the day is,
How hot the scent is of the summer rose,
How dreadful the black wastes of evening sky,
How dreadful the tall soldiers drumming by.

But we have speech, to chill the angry day,   5
And speech, to dull the rose's cruel scent.
We spell away the overhanging night,
We spell away the soldiers and the fright.

There's a cool web of language winds us in,
Retreat from too much joy or too much fear: 10
We grow sea-green at last and coldly die
In brininess and volubility.

But if we let our tongues lose self-possession,
Throwing off language and its watery clasp
Before our death, instead of when death comes,   15
Facing the wide glare of the children's day,
Facing the rose, the dark sky and the drums,
We shall go mad no doubt and die that way.

ROBERT GRAVES

1   'Speech and dumbness appear to represent two contrasted outlooks on life.' Do you agree?

2   What ambiguity of feeling is revealed by the identification of speech with both 'volubility' (line 12) and 'self-possession' (line 13)?

3   Explore the relationship between the quality of the pictures and the poet's style in stanza 1. How are the pictures modified in stanza 2?

4   Can the repetitions in the first two stanzas be justified?

5   'Simplicity of tone masking complexity of ideas.' Is this a fair comment? Does it reject the possibility of harmony between theme and tone?

6   Attempt to reconstruct the marine imagery alluded to in the title and in the third and fourth stanzas. Is it a) accurate (i.e. does it establish a true parallel?) and b) appropriate in this context?

THE BARDS

The bards falter in shame, their running verse
Stumbles, with marrow-bones the drunken diners
Pelt them for their delay.
It is a something fearful in the song
Plagues them—an unknown grief that like a churl   5
Goes commonplace in cowskin
And bursts unheralded, crowing and coughing,
An unpilled holly-club twirled in his hand,
Into their many-shielded, samite-curtained,
Jewel-bright hall where twelve kings sit at chess   10
Over the white-bronze pieces and the gold;
And by a gross enchantment
Flails down the rafters and leads off the queens—
The wild-swan-breasted, the rose-ruddy-cheeked
Raven-haired daughters of their admiration—   15
To stir his black pots and to bed on straw.

ROBERT GRAVES

1   Does this poem make a statement of universal application, or is its appeal limited to the evocation of a particular historical period?

2   What is the theme of the poem?

3   Comment on its descriptive qualities.

4   How is the tone affected by word-play and pastiche (the imitation of Old English verse, *e.g.* compounds like *jewel-bright* and the alliteration of lines 6–7)?

5   'The contrast between order and lawlessness is underlined by diction and rhythm.' Attempt an evaluation of this statement.

William Wordsworth and Robert Frost ensure that they achieve the right degree of objectivity in the expression of private feeling by creating *personae*: the 'Boy' in the extract from *The Prelude* (A), and the 'He' of the poem 'The Most of It' (B). In each poem we may sense that a memorable experience is being relived. The Winander episode is presented by Wordsworth as one of the turning points in his own spiritual journey; and Frost's poem seems to recall an equally important moment, though 'The Most of It', being a twentieth-century, and post-Darwinian, poem conveys a sadder and less optimistic view of existence than Wordsworth's.

A

There was a Boy: ye knew him well, ye cliffs
And islands of Winander!—many a time
At evening, when the earliest stars began
To move along the edges of the hills,
Rising or setting, would he stand alone   5
Beneath the trees or by the glimmering lake,
And there, with fingers interwoven, both hands
Pressed closely palm to palm, and to his mouth
Uplifted, he, as through an instrument,
Blew mimic hootings to the silent owls,   10
That they might answer him; and they would shout
Across the watery Vale, and shout again,
Responsive to his call, with quivering peals,

And long halloos, and screams, and echoes loud
Redoubled and redoubled; concourse wild   15
Of mirth and jocund din! And when it chanced
That pauses of deep silence mock'd his skill,
Then sometimes, in that silence, while he hung
Listening, a gentle shock of mild surprise
Has carried far into his heart the voice   20
Of mountain torrents; or the visible scene
Would enter unawares into his mind
With all its solemn imagery, its rocks,
Its woods, and that uncertain Heaven, receiv'd
Into the bosom of the steady Lake.   25

WILLIAM WORDSWORTH

1   'The poet has mixed feelings about the Boy.' Do you agree?
2   . . . ye knew him well, ye cliffs
     And islands of Winander!

     . . . and to his mouth
     Uplifted, he, as through an instrument,
     Blew mimic hootings to the silent owls,
     That they might answer him . . .

     . . . a gentle shock of mild surprise
     Has carried far into his heart the voice
     Of mountain torrents . . .

     How can the differences of tone in these extracts be accounted
     for? Are they unconscious or deliberate?—If deliberate, what
     function does the variation fulfil?
3   Consider the effectiveness in their contexts of the following
     words and phrases:
          the repeated 'and' (lines 7–16), shout (line 11), jocund din
          (line 16), deep (line 17), hung (line 18), far (line 21), heart (line
          21), bosom (line 25).
4   Consider the verse-form chosen for the long poem from which
     this passage is taken. Does blank verse emphasize or help to conceal
     changes of tone?

5   Make a detailed examination of the structure of the passage.

6   'The effectiveness of these lines springs from the deliberate creation of a false climax as a prelude to a true climax.' Attempt an evaluation of this statement.

B

THE MOST OF IT

He thought he kept the universe alone;
For all the voice in answer he could wake
Was but the mocking echo of his own
From some tree-hidden cliff across the lake.
Some morning from the boulder-broken beach   5
He would cry out on life, that what it wants
Is not its own love back in copy speech,
But counter-love, original response.
And nothing ever came of what he cried
Unless it was the embodiment that crashed   10
In the cliff's talus on the other side,
And then in the far distant water splashed,
But after a time allowed for it to swim,
Instead of proving human when it neared
And someone else additional to him,   15
As a great buck it powerfully appeared,
Pushing the crumpled water up ahead,
And landed pouring like a waterfall,
And stumbled through the rocks with horny tread,
And forced the underbrush—and that was all.   20

ROBERT FROST

1   What is the poet's attitude towards the 'He' of this incident? What stylistic features reveal this attitude?

2   The buck (line 16) seems to have a special significance in the poem. Would it be possible to describe the poet's experience without using this symbol?

3   Try to explain the distinction between 'its own love back' (line 7) and 'counter-love, original response' (line 8).

4   'Slipshod diction thinly disguised by the formality of the verse-form.' Consider this view of the poem's style.

5   What attitude towards the buck is implied in the words 'stumbled', 'horny' and 'forced' (lines 19–20)?

6   Examine the use of 'and' in lines 18–20.

COMPARATIVE STUDY

1   Compare the two attitudes to nature conveyed in the lines from The Prelude and the poem by Robert Frost.

2   'Both poets have used considerable skill in reproducing a poetic experience under cover of an almost naive simplicity.' Discuss.

TWELVE

In SEVEN, we saw how Hopkins owed something to the spirit of George Herbert without being indebted to him stylistically. Here is another example of the influence that Herbert had on later admirers— in this case Ella Wheeler Wilcox who, in 'Guerdon', seems to imitate the style of writing we find in 'Life'.

A

(In 'Spring and Fall' (page 47) we have already encountered a device which Hopkins might have become acquainted with in 'Life', i.e. the creation of an imaginary dramatic situation to act as a setting for the metaphor through which the poetic experience is conveyed.)

LIFE

I made a posy, while the day ran by:
Here will I smell my remnant out, and tie
    My life within this band.
But time did beckon to the flowers, and they
By noon most cunningly did steal away,   5
    And wither'd in my hand.

My hand was next to them, and then my heart;
I took, without more thinking, in good part
    Time's gentle admonition;

Who did so sweetly death's sad taste convey,   10
Making my mind to smell my fatal day,
    Yet sugring the suspicion.

Farewell, dear flowers, sweetly your time ye spent,
Fit, while ye liv'd, for smell or ornament,
    And after death for cures.   15
I follow straight without complaints or grief,
Since if my scent be good, I care not, if
    It be as short as yours.

GEORGE HERBERT

1   'An idea and a metaphor constantly intertwining'—Consider
this view of the poem.

2   Cunningly (line 5), in good part (line 8), sad (line 10), sugring
(line 12), dear (line 13), fit (line 14), ornament (line 14), good (line
17).
    Can these words and phrases, in their contexts, be defended
from the criticism that they are commonplaces, not the language of
poetry?

3   By examining the diction, imagery and tone, try to decide
whether or not Herbert has succeeded in reproducing a poetic
experience.

4   What effect has the use of personification had on the tone?—
Has it enhanced or detracted from the quality of the experience?

5   Discuss the rhyme scheme and the use of short lines.

B

GUERDON

Upon the white cheek of the Cherub year
    I saw a tear.

Alas! I murmured, that the Year should borrow
    So soon a sorrow.
Just then the sunlight fell with sudden flame: 5
    The tear became
A wondrous diamond sparkling in the light—
    A beauteous sight.

Upon my soul there fell such woeful loss,
    I said, 'The cross   10
Is grievous for a life as young as mine.'
    Just then, like wine,
God's sunlight shone from His high Heavens down;
    And lo! a crown
Gleamed in the place of what I thought a burden—   15
    My sorrow's guerdon.

ELLA WHEELER WILCOX

1   Paying special attention to structure, consider the interplay between experience and its figurative expression in this poem.

2   'The chief merit of the poem is its appeal to the senses.' Do you agree?

3   Attempt to justify the use of the following words and phrases in their contexts:

    borrow (line 3), just then (lines 5 and 12), light (line 7).

4   Discuss the use of short lines.

COMPARATIVE STUDY

1   Assuming that Ella Wheeler Wilcox had read 'Life', would it be reasonable to suggest that she appreciated George Herbert's aims and achievement?

2   'Life' tries to reach our feelings through the senses and seems to appeal to the reason only as an afterthought. 'Guerdon' appeals primarily to the reason.' Do you agree?

3   Which poem do you prefer?

THIRTEEN

Which of the following translations of a chorus from Sophocles's
Oedipus at Colonus do you prefer?

A

To a land, stranger, of noble horses,
The fairest of earth's abodes thou comest,
To white-gleaming Colonus, where
Nightingales ever love to haunt
Trilling loudly their liquid carols   5
Hidden close in the green groves,
Dwelling midst of the wine-dark ivy,
The God's bower inviolate
Rich with a myriad fruits and unvisited
By sun, where never fierce storms   10
Of wind bluster, and where the reveller
Dionysus is ever wont to wander
Companioned by the Nymphs that nursed him.

And there, wet with the dew of heaven,
Narcissus in lovely clusters morn by   15
Morn is blooming, the ancient crown
Of those great Goddesses; there the yellow
Sheen of crocus; and there in sleepless
Never minishing streams and rills
Kephisus spreadeth his vagrant water;   20
And each day with his unstained flood

Over the plains of the land's swelling bosom
He moveth, ever bestowing
Quick fertility—haunts frequented
By quires of the Muses and the golden-
reined chariot of Aphrodite.   25

R. C. TREVELYAN

B

Here, where the Warrior Steed had birth,
    Come wanderer, to a place of rest,
A home, the dearest upon earth,
    Beneath Colonus' gleaming crest.
Often a secret music through this vale   5
Comes thrilling, where some sweet-voiced nightingale
    Hides in a dell of green;
She loves the clustering ivy, dark as wine,
And that deep-leaved, that thousand-berried shrine,
Where no foot treads, where never sun may shine   10
    Nor storm-wind pierce the screen.
Only the mystic Dionysus there,
Ringed by the nymphs who erst his cradle bare,
    Treadeth his dance unseen.

Here blossoms in fresh dew from heaven   15
    The crocus with its gleam of gold,
And clusters of narcissus, given
    As crowns by men of old
To Maid and Mother, goddesses most high;
Nor ever run those sleepless channels dry   20
    Which shepherds o'er the plain
The runlets of Cephisus; day by day
Through earth's deep bosom he will wind his way,

And swift her life increaseth, whereso stray
   Those waters without stain;   25
A haunt not hated by the Muses' band,
Nor turneth Aphrodite from this land
   Averse her golden rein.

GILBERT MURRAY

C

The land of running horses, fair
Colonus takes a guest;
He shall not seek another home,
For this, in all the earth and air,
Is most secure and loveliest.   5

In the god's untrodden vale
Where leaves and berries throng,
And wine-dark ivy climbs the bough,
The sweet, sojourning nightingale
Murmurs all night long.   10

No sun nor wind may enter there
Nor the winter's rain;
But ever through the shadow goes
Dionysus reveller,
Immortal maenads in his train.   15

Here with drops of heaven's dews
At Daybreak all the year,
The clusters of narcissus bloom,
Time-hallowed garlands for the brows
Of those great ladies whom we fear.   20

The crocus like a little sun
Blooms with its yellow ray;
The river's fountains are awake,
And his nomadic streams that run
Unthinned forever, and never stay;   25

But like perpetual lovers move
On the maternal land.
And here the choiring Muses come,
And the divinity of love
With gold reins in her hand.   30

ROBERT FITZGERALD

FOURTEEN

John Dryden would have disliked the poems that follow, just as he disliked the poetry of John Donne, of whom he wrote: 'He perplexes the minds of the fair sex with nice speculations of philosophy, when he should engage their hearts, and entertain them with the softnesses of love'. George Barker might well have had this kind of attitude in mind when he chose 'Love Poem' as a provocative—though not misleading—title; and Andrew Marvell might have aroused certain expectations in his first readers which, at first glance, his poem 'A Definition of Love' seems to leave unsatisfied. Both poets communicate their experience of life in terms which they probably first encountered in a lecture-room or in a treatise on astronomy; but an examination of their poems may bring us to the conclusion that Dryden was wrong in thinking that the language of intellectual adventures and the language of feeling are incompatible.

A

(A modern atlas is a collection of *planispheres* (line 24) i.e. projections of spheres, like the Earth, on a plane. *Conjunction* (line 31) and *opposition* (line 32) have an astronomical significance, which is included here with their more familiar meanings. Planets or stars are 'in conjunction' when they are close to each other, and 'in opposition' when exactly opposite, as seen from the earth's surface.)

THE DEFINITION OF LOVE

I

My Love is of a birth as rare
As 'tis for object strange and high:
It was begotten by despair
Upon impossibility.

II

Magnanimous Despair alone   5
Could show me so divine a thing,
Where feeble Hope could Ne'r have flown
But vainly flapt its Tinsel Wing.

III

And yet I quickly might arrive
Where my extended Soul is fixt,   10
But Fate does Iron wedges drive,
And alwaies crouds it self betwixt.

IV

For Fate with jealous Eye does see
Two perfect Loves; nor lets them close:
Their union would her ruine be,   15
And her Tyrannick pow'r depose.

V

And therefore her Decrees of Steel
Us as the distant Poles have plac'd,
(Though Loves whole World on us doth wheel)
Not by themselves to be embrac'd.   20

VI

Unless the giddy Heaven fall,
And Earth some new Convulsion tear;
And, us to joyn, the World should all
Be cramp'd into a Planisphere.

VII

As Lines so Loves oblique may well   25
Themselves in every Angle greet:
But ours so truly Paralel,
Though infinite can never meet.

VIII

Therefore the Love which us doth bind,
But Fate so enviously debarrs,   30
Is the Conjunction of the Mind,
And Opposition of the Stars.

ANDREW MARVELL

1   Discuss the thematic significance of Law in this poem.

2   'The poet has shown great skill in bringing together visual and non-visual, latent and fully developed images.' Discuss.

3   Analyse the structure of the poem.

4   Consider the relationship between the diction and the scientific imagery of the last four stanzas.

5   Consider the following words in their contexts. Do you think they were well chosen?

high (line 2), Tinsel (line 8), depose (line 16), giddy (line 21), greet (line 26).

B

The astronomical ideas and practice of the past as well as the modern science are alluded to in George Barker's poem.

An *astrolable* (line 15) was an instrument used for taking altitudes and for solving other problems of astronomy; and in the first two lines there seems to be a reference to the idea of the planets fixed in spheres which rotated together.

Parallax (line 6) denotes the apparent displacement of an object due to the changed position of the observer. (The allusion here seems to be to the passing of time as measured by the rotation of the earth.)

In the first stanza there is an allusion to light years; and in the personification here there may be a passing reference to the red colour of certain galaxies when observed through a powerful telescope, a phenomenon some astronomers interpret as an indication that they are rapidly receding from us. The poet seems to be drawing on the idea that, owing to the distances involved and the speed at which light travels, astronomers with powerful telescopes may observe 'events' in space which were actually coincident in time with phases of our own historical past.

Vocable (line 12) is synonymous with 'word'.

Antimony (line 16) is a contradiction in a law or between laws.

LOVE POEM

Where the kissing systems turn
  Arm in arm across the sky
And the sleepless years return
Red-eyed, haunted, to their high
  Stations in astronomy: 5

There, shaking water at parallax,
  Lolling along distances,
The morning lets the stars relax
And makes a magic among tenses:
  Love rises from her bed of senses.   10

The systems, wheeling in degrees,
  Speak in eternal vocables:
'The heart, through all its allegories,
Shall always walk the stellar alleys
  Clasping an astrolabe of troubles'.   15

Thus, crosswise on antinomies,
  The angel and the anthropoid,
The wrongs and the responsibilities
  Making love across the void
  Kiss in a shower of pities.   20

GEORGE BARKER

1   What differences of perspective has the poet tried to establish
between stanzas 1 and 2? Consider the parts played by imagery and
diction in creating a harmony between them.

2   In what sense are the stars allowed to *relax* (line 8)?

3   Consider the thematic significance of the contrast between the
different ideas of Time in:

      And makes a magic among tenses (line 9)
  and   Speak in eternal vocables (line 12).

4   Suggest an interpretation of lines 13–15.

5   Consider the relation of the concluding stanza to the preceding
ones. Has the ground been prepared for this statement of the human
predicament?

6   Does the scientific imagery help or hinder the poet in his
attempt to reproduce a poetic experience?

7   Consider the following words in their contexts. Do you think
they were well chosen?

      sleepless (line 3), vocables (line 12), alleys (line 14), shower
      (line 20).

COMPARATIVE STUDY

1   Examine the means by which Andrew Marvell and George
Barker have tried to soften the impact of their learned imagery. Have
they both been successful?

2   'Attempts to relate the microcosm of man to the macrocosm
of the universe invariably end in bathos.'

      'When the normal privacy and littleness of human experience

are measured on the scale of the universal the effect is one of great poignancy.'

Try to evaluate these statements in the light of the two poems.

3   Do the seventeenth-century and twentieth-century poets share a vision of life, or only an interest in astronomy?

4   Was Dryden right or wrong?

FIFTEEN

The following passages have been extracted from T. S. Eliot's 'Ash Wednesday', a poem about spiritual death and regeneration. The symbolism of *A* is in part personal, e.g.

> The Lady is withdrawn
> In a white gown, to contemplation, in a white gown

—the Lady being a nun who represents spiritual health throughout the poem. Other symbols, like the juniper tree and the dry bones, are public property, having been taken from two passages in the Old Testament.

In B, the imagery of the first two sections is of the kind we might encounter in dreams; while the 'maytime' image seems to owe something to the world of Chaucer and medieval romance.

A

Lady, three white leopards sat under a juniper-tree
In the cool of the day, having fed to satiety
On my legs my heart my liver and that which had been
    contained
In the hollow round of my skull. And God said
Shall these bones live? shall these   5
Bones live? And that which had been contained
In the bones (which were already dry) said chirping:
Because of the goodness of this Lady
And because of her loveliness, and because
She honours the Virgin in meditation,
We shine with brightness. And I who am here dissembled   10

Proffer my deeds to oblivion, and my love
To the posterity of the desert and the fruit of the gourd.
It is this which recovers
My guts the strings of my eyes and the indigestible portions   15
Which the leopards reject. The Lady is withdrawn
In a white gown, to contemplation, in a white gown.
Let the whiteness of bones atone to forgetfulness.
There is no life in them. As I am forgotten
And would be forgotten, so I would forget   20
Thus devoted, concentrated in purpose. And God said
Prophesy to the wind, to the wind only for only
The wind will listen. And the bones sang chirping
With the burden of the grasshopper . . .

T. S. ELIOT

These are the Old Testament passages alluded to in A:

1

And Ahab told Jezebel all that Elijah had done, and withal how
he had slain all the prophets with the sword. Then Jezebel sent a
messenger unto Elijah, saying, So let the gods do to me, and more
also, if I make not thy life as the life of one of them by tomorrow
about this time. And when he saw that, he arose, and went for his
life, and came to Beer-sheba, which belongeth to Judah, and left his
servant there.

But he himself went a day's journey into the wilderness, and came
and sat down under a juniper tree: and he requested for himself that
he might die; and said, It is enough; now, O Lord, take away my
life; for I am not better than my fathers. And as he lay and slept
under a juniper tree, behold, then an angel touched him, and said
unto him, Arise and eat. And he looked, and, behold, there was a cake
baked on the coals, and a cruse of water at his head. And he did eat
and drink, and laid him down again. And the angel of the Lord came
again the second time, and touched him, and said, Arise and eat;
because the journey is too great for thee. And he arose, and did eat,
and drink, and went in the strength of that meat forty days and forty
nights unto Horeb the mount of God.

                                                    I Kings, xix, 1–8.

2

The hand of the Lord was upon me, and carried me out in the spirit of the Lord, and set me down in the midst of the valley which was full of bones, and caused me to pass by them round about: and, behold, there were very many in the open valley; and, lo, they were very dry. And he said unto me, Son of man, can these bones live? And I answered, O Lord God, thou knowest. Again he said unto me, Prophesy upon these bones, and say unto them, O ye dry bones, hear the word of the Lord. Thus saith the Lord God unto these bones; Behold, I will cause breath to enter into you, and ye shall live: And I will lay sinews upon you, and will bring up flesh upon you, and cover you with skin, and put breath in you, and ye shall live; and ye shall know that I am the Lord. So I prophesied as I was commanded: and as I prophesied, there was a noise, and behold a shaking, and the bones came together, bone to his bone. And when I beheld, lo, the sinews and the flesh came up upon them, and the skin covered them above: but there was no breath in them. Then said he unto me, Prophesy unto the wind, prophesy, son of man, and say to the wind, Thus saith the Lord God; Come from the four winds, O breath, and breathe upon those slain, that they may live. So I prophesied as he commanded me, and the breath came into them, and they lived, and stood up upon their feet, an exceeding great army.

Ezekiel, xxxvii, 1–10.

1   Bearing in mind the poem's title, 'Ash Wednesday' (this is the beginning of the forty-day period of Lent and, liturgically, the day set aside for meditation on death), can you discover Eliot's reasons for quoting these particular passages?

2   What is the significance of the contrast between the meals associated with Elijah's and with Eliot's juniper trees?

3   Consider Eliot's use of Ezekiel's 'Prophesy unto the wind'. How does he use it to make a statement of his own about *a*) spiritual, and *b*) social concerns? Do these lines contain any other symbols designed to confront us with a paradox?

4   What does *Thus* refer to in line 21?

5   Consider the role of 'the Lady'.

6   How does the repeated use of the word 'white' influence the meaning of these lines?

7   Is the tone pessimistic or optimistic? Try to define the nature of the experience reflected here.

8   To what extent has Eliot been influenced by the style of the King James bible?

9   Consider the use of *dissembled* (line 11) and *recovers* (line 14).

10   Could Eliot be defended against the criticism that he had been unnecessarily repetitive?

11   Can the absence of punctuation in line 3 be justified?

B

At the first turning of the second stair
I turned and saw below
The same shape twisted on the banister
Under the vapour in the fetid air
Struggling with the devil of the stairs who wears   5
The deceitful face of hope and of despair.

At the second turning of the second stair
I left them twisting, turning below;
There were no more faces and the stair was dark,
Damp, jagged, like an old man's mouth drivelling,   10
    beyond repair,
Or the toothed gullet of an aged shark.

At the second turning of the third stair
Was a slotted window bellied like the fig's fruit
And beyond the hawthorn blossom and a pasture scene
The broadbacked figure drest in blue and green   15
Enchanted the maytime with an antique flute.

Blown hair is sweet, brown hair over the mouth blown,
Lilac and brown hair;
Distraction, music of the flute, stops and steps of the mind
   over the third stair,
Fading, fading; strength beyond hope and despair   20
Climbing the third stair.

T. S. ELIOT

1   Suggest an explanation of the staircase symbolism.

2   Can you think of a reason for the precise details about the poet's progress up the staircase (lines 1, 7, 12)?

3   Can you see any link between the allegorical form of this section of the poem and the medieval imagery it contains?

4   Attempt an explanation of the paradox in line 6.

5   Why has Eliot introduced the idea of old age into the similes in lines 10 and 11?

6   What does the maytime garden represent?

7   Explore the influence of a) structure (both of the extract in general and of individual sentences) and b) diction, in making the garden seem attractive.

8   Consider the implications of

        stops and steps of the mind over the third stair (line 19).

9   Is the maytime garden a positive or negative element in this allegory?

The two extracts have been taken from consecutive 'movements' of a poem composed in six sections.

1   Consider the contrast between the vision of animal life communicated in A and that of B, lines 4–11.

2   Examine the role of colour in the two extracts.

3   What poetic statement has Eliot tried to make by presenting the symbols of B after those of A?

4   What do you consider to be the chief advantages (or disadvantages) of the poetic technique represented by these passages?

PART 2   The criticism of prose

INTRODUCTION

The passages that follow have been taken fron novels published
between 1911 and 1927: D. H. Lawrence's first novel, The White
Peacock (1911), E. M. Forster's A Passage to India (1924), and Virginia
Woolf's To the Lighthouse (1927). Apart from varying degrees of
imaginative range and the different areas of experience he is inclined
to explore, a novelist is distinguished by his own 'voice', which
reflects his particular mode of sensibility, his attitudes towards
characters and events (and also towards his reader), as well as his
particular solution to the problem of controlling a body of imaginative material which must emerge with the imprint of a unified view
of life. In the commentary that follows each passage, it is hoped to
reveal how a writer stamps his personality on imagined events, and
creates such a voice for himself.

(1)

They decided to bury him in our churchyard at Greymede
under the beeches; the widow would have it so, and nothing
might be denied her in her state.

It was a magnificent morning in early spring when I watched
among the trees to see the procession come down the hillside.   5
The upper air was woven with the music of the larks, and my
whole world thrilled with the conception of the summer. The
young pale wind-flowers had arisen by the woodgale, and
under the hazels, when perchance the hot sun pushed his way,
new little suns dawned, and blazed with real light. There was a   10
certain thrill and quickening everywhere, as a woman must feel
when she has conceived. A sallow tree in a favoured spot
looked like a pale gold cloud of summer dawn; nearer it had
poised a golden fairy busby on every twig, and was voiced with
a hum of bees, like any sacred golden bush, uttering its gladness 15
in the sacred murmur of bees, and in warm scent. Birds called

and flashed on every hand; they made off exultant with
streaming strands of grass, or wisps of fleece, plunging into the
dark spaces of the wood and out again into the blue.

A lad moved across the field from the farm below with a   20
dog, no a fussy, black-legged lamb trotting along on his toes,
with its tail swinging behind. They were going to the mothers
on the common, who moved like little grey clouds among the
dark gorse.

I cannot help forgetting, and sharing the spink's triumph,   25
when he flashes past with a fleece from a bramble bush. It will
cover the bedded moss, it will weave among the soft red
cowhair beautifully. It is a prize, it is an ecstasy to have
captured it at the right moment, and the nest is nearly ready.

Ah, but the thrush is scornful, ringing out his voice from   30
the hedge! He sets his breast against the mud, and models it
warm for the turquoise eggs—blue, blue, bluest of eggs, which
cluster so close and round against the breast, which round up
beneath the breast, nestling content. You should see the bright
ecstasy in the eyes of a nesting thrush, because of the rounded   35
caress of the eggs against her breast!

What a hurry the jenny wren makes—hoping I shall not see
her dart into the low bush. I have a delight in watching them
against their shy little wills. But they have all risen with a
rush of wings, and gone, the birds. The air is brushed with   40
agitation. There is no lark in the sky, not one; the heaven is
clear of wings or twinkling dot——.

Till the heralds come—the heralds wave like shadows in
the bright air, crying, lamenting, fretting forever. Rising and
falling and circling round and round, the slow-waving   45
peewits cry and complain and lift their broad wings in sorrow.
They stoop suddenly to the ground, the lapwings, then in
another throb of anguish and protest, they swing up again,
offering a glistening white breast to the sunlight, to deny it in
black shadow, then a glisten of green, and all the time crying   50
and crying in despair.

The pheasants are frightened into cover, they run and dart
through the hedge. The cold cock must fly in his haste,
spread himself on his streaming plumes, and sail into the
wood's security.   55

There is a cry in answer to the peewits, echoing louder and
stronger the lamentation of the lapwings, a wail which hushes
the birds. The men come over the brow of the hill slowly,
with the old squire walking tall and straight in front; six
bowed men bearing the coffin on their shoulders, treading   60
heavily and cautiously, under the great weight of the glistening
white coffin; six men following behind, ill at ease, waiting
their turn for the burden. You can see the red handkerchiefs
knotted round the throats, and their shirt-fronts blue and
white between the open waistcoats. The coffin is of new   65
unpolished wood, gleaming and glistening in the sunlight; the
men who carry it remember all their lives the smell of new,
warm elm-wood.

Again a loud cry from the hill-top. The woman has followed
thus far, the big, shapeless woman, and she cries with loud cries   70
after the white coffin as it descends the hill, and the children
that cling to her skirts weep aloud, and are not to be hushed
by the other woman, who bends over them, but does not form
one of the group. How the crying frightens the birds, and the
rabbits; and the lambs away there run to their mothers. But   75
the peewits are not frightened, they add their notes to the
sorrow; they circle after the white, retreating coffin, they circle
round the woman; it is they who forever 'keen' the sorrows of
this world. They are like priests in their robes, more black
than white, more grief than hope, driving endlessly round and   80
round, turning, lifting, falling and crying always in mournful
desolation, repeating their last syllables like the broken
accents of despair.

The bearers have at last sunk between the high banks, and
turned out of sight. The big woman cannot see them, and yet   85
she stands to look. She must go home, there is nothing left.

They have rested the coffin on the gate posts, and the bearers
are wiping the sweat from their faces. They put their hands
to their shoulders on the place where the weight has pressed.

The other six are placing the pads on their shoulders,   90
when a girl comes up with a jug, and a blue pot. The squire
drinks first and fills for the rest. Meanwhile the girl stands
back under the hedge, away from the coffin which smells of
new elm-wood. In imagination she pictures the man shut up

there in close darkness, while the sunlight flows all outside, 95
and she catches her breast with terror. She must turn and
rustle among the leaves of the violets for the flowers she does
not see. Then, trembling, she comes to herself, and plucks a
few flowers and breathes them hungrily into her soul, for
comfort. The men put down the pots beside her, with thanks, 100
and the squire gives the word. The bearers lift the burden
again, and the elm-boughs rattle along the hollow white wood,
and the pitiful red clusters of elm-flowers sweep along it,
always the compassionate buds in their fulness of life bend
down to comfort the dark man shut up there. 'Perhaps,' the 105
girl thinks, 'he hears them, and goes softly to sleep.' She
shakes the tears out of her eyes on to the ground and, taking
up her pots, goes slowly down, over the brooks.

In a while, I too got up and went down to the mill, which
lay red and peaceful, with the blue smoke rising as winsomely 110
and carelessly as ever. On the other side of the valley I could
see a pair of horses nod slowly across the fallow, in the still,
lonely valley, full of sunshine and eternal forgetfulness. The
day had already forgotten. The water was blue and white and
dark-burnished with shadows; two swans sailed across the 115
reflected trees with perfect blithe grace; the gloom that had
passed across was gone. I watched the swan with his ruffled
wings swell onwards; I watched his slim consort go peeping
into corners and under bushes; I saw him steer clear of the
bushes, to keep full in view, turning his head to me imperi- 120
ously, till I longed to pelt him with the empty husks of last
year's flowers, knapweed and scabious. I was too indolent, and
I turned instead to the orchard.

There the daffodils were lifting their heads and throwing
back their yellow curls. At the foot of each sloping, grey old 125
tree stood a family of flowers, some bursten with golden
fulness, some lifting their heads slightly, to show a modest,
sweet countenance, others still hiding their faces, leaning
forward pensively from the jaunty grey-green spears; I wished
I had their language, to talk to them distinctly. 130

Overhead, the trees, with lifted fingers shook out their hair
to the sun decking themselves with buds as white and cool as a
water-nymph's breasts.

I began to be very glad. The colts-foot discs glowed and
laughed in a merry company down the path; I stroked the   135
velvet faces and laughed also, and I smelled the scent of black-
currant leaves, which is full of childish memories. The house
was quiet and complacent; it was peopled by ghosts again, but
the ghosts had only come to enjoy the warm place once more,
carrying sunshine in their arms and scattering it through the   140
dusk of gloomy rooms.

D. H. LAWRENCE, The White Peacock

Reading the above passage, one is tempted to put oneself in the place
of the publisher confronted half a century ago by this work from an
unknown author. We know that the right decision was reached;
but what was the first reaction to these pages? Did someone sense
that here he had stumbled upon a potentially great writer, or was he
too busy suppressing pangs of outrage—at the clumsiness of line 25;
at the attempt made to seize him by the scruff of the neck in line 34;
at the nursery register of 'How the crying frightens the birds, and the
rabbits'; at the sentimental Easter-card picture of the daffodils'
'yellow curls' (line 125)?

It isn't very hard to pick holes in this extract—and it contains a
more serious technical fault than any of those yet quoted. But if we
take the trouble to read it a second or third time we may discover
that its shortcomings recede into insignificance. This will depend on
how much sympathy we have with a writer who is beginning to test
the tools at his disposal; and on whether or not we agree with the
lines from the Essay on Criticism quoted on the title page of this book.
If we are prepared to give Lawrence the benefit of the doubt, what
is the 'End', or intention, that Pope would have advised us to look
for?

The White Peacock is a first-person novel about childhood, youth and
early manhood. Here, the narrator is describing the funeral procession of his friend, the gamekeeper, on a morning in spring. As his
choice of season suggests, Lawrence is trying to show how an
awareness of what dying means can be reached simultaneously with
an awakening to the delight of the senses. The three movements of
the passage point the contrast between the events of the spring day
and the inert body of the dead man who provides the excuse for

the description and is, significantly, the most easily forgotten part
of it.

In the first movement (corresponding to the first six paragraphs),
the keynote is birth, preceded by conception, which suggests the
comparisons in lines 7 and 10. Birds are nesting; a black lamb
appears in the valley; sheep are referred to as 'the mothers on the
common' (lines 22–3). With the renewal of animal life comes the fresh
budding of plants and the 'birth' of the day: a tree looks like 'a
pale gold cloud of summer dawn' (line 13). The second movement is
dominated by the funeral procession. The lamentation of the widow
is echoed by the 'keening' of the peewits. That this movement is an
interruption of the prevailing mood of the passage is emphasized by
the uneasiness of the men waiting their turn to carry the coffin
(line 62), by the fact that the implied protest in the woman's
behaviour is made explicit in the description of the birds (line 48),
and by the terror of the girl who appears with refreshments for
the men It is the girl's readiness to seek relief from frightening
thoughts that consigns the dead man to oblivion and makes a
bridge between the second and last movements (lines 96–108). In the
last, the narrator becomes absorbed again in the spring day. He
begins 'to be very glad' (line 134), and the event which has inspired
this jubilate is recalled only in the husks of dead flowers (lines 121–2)
and the ghosts with which an idle fancy peoples the rooms of the
empty house (line 138).

D. H. Lawrence must have approved of that famous account of
empathy contained in one of Keats's letters: '. . . if a Sparrow come
before my Window I take part in its existence and peck about the
Gravel', for it is his willingness to do just this that makes the extract
memorable. Sensation, he seems to be telling us, is the lingua franca of
all forms of life; and to observe (as he does very accurately) is to
identify himself not only with the men who are going to 'remember
all their lives the smell of new, warm elm-wood' (lines 66–7), but
also with the thrush in the act of hatching its eggs (line 31). The
underlying irony of the passage is that the gamekeeper is quite
apart from such sympathetic leaps of the imagination: the girl
attempts to bridge the gap, fails, and retreats to find consolation in
the scent of violets; and the clumsy syntax of line 25 is the result of
Lawrence's wish to convey simultaneously the narrator's failure to
concentrate on the fact of death, and his exultant awareness of the

life around him: 'I cannot help forgetting [that the gamekeeper is dead], and sharing the spink's triumph.' There follows an elaborate attempt to disguise this disloyalty, first in the pathetic fallacy which turns the peewits into mourners and then in the theatrical description of the widow and children, and the staging of the funeral procession as a rather crude dramatic tableau.

It is under the heading 'perspective' that the purist is most likely to quarrel with this passage. We must therefore try to fix the position of the 'I' of the narrative, i.e. the fictitious hero who is projecting himself back into youth and recapturing the emotions of the spring morning. When we do so we discover that Lawrence and his *persona* (the 'I' of the narrative) sometimes merge and become indistinguishable from one another: for example, in the middle of an account of what the narrator has seen and heard we are given glimpses of the inner experience of the men with the coffin, and of the girl, which only the all-knowing novelist can provide ('remember all their lives'; ' "Perhaps," the girl thinks, "he hears them and goes softly to sleep" '—*lines* 105–6). In this case, the fusion of identities has been heralded by an unexpected use of the zoom lens, for the looking-down-on-the-valley stance has allowed us such details as the men's check shirts, the glistening elm-wood and the blue pot. A further confusion, this time a stylistic one, results from the occasional merging of the young-man narrator and the actual youth (his former self) who is sitting on the hill-side. 'What a hurry the jenny wren makes' (*line* 37) has a childish register; in contrast, 'more black than white, more grief than hope' (*lines* 79–80) has a terse, manly eloquence. One can sympathize with D. H. Lawrence's dilemma. He is not prepared to deprive himself of the novelist's total view of the scene, or the adult's awareness of what is going on. But the very strength of the passage comes from the fact that the boy also is in it. This has been its keynote, justifying the use of 'mothers' where we might otherwise have expected 'sheep'; preparing the way for the flight of fancy that makes the elm-buds 'compassionate' (*line* 104); above all, providing the excuse for the whole pagan hymn which explodes out of the otherwise perplexing use of *sacred* in lines 15 and 16. The 'voice' here is that of a writer who, though failing to achieve that complete identification with his narrator which would have made the passage technically watertight, none the less finds himself sufficiently released through the persona of the youth to proclaim his own trusting, uninhibited and essentially youthful acceptance of life.

The passage's weaknesses, then, may be seen as the obverse side of great virtues. The failure of identification, the breaks in the perspective and lapses of style are the price paid for a brave unselfconsciousness that sweeps us along so that we never really doubt that this writer is big enough to use such emotive words as *magnificent, blazed, exultant, terror* and *soul*. One of the features of the passage that helps to convince us of this fact is its utterly confident sensuousness, and the accurate observation it contains: the *rattle* of elm-boughs on the coffin (line 102), the *mournful desolation* of the peewits' cry (lines 81-2), the *grey-green spears* of daffodils before they bloom (line 129). The description of the thrush—which stretches prose to its limits—is typically courageous: 'He sets his breast against the mud, and models it warm for the turquoise eggs—blue, blue, bluest of eggs, which cluster so close and round against the breast, which round up beneath the breast, nestling content' (lines 31-4). We are made to feel the warm mud moulded to the shape of the bird, to feel the roundness of the eggs and see their precise colour: turquoise; while the repeated 'blue, blue, bluest' conveys the excitement of the boy who has discovered them, and the repetitions of 'round' and 'breast' invite us to share even the sensations of the sitting bird.

The elasticity of this fresh and responsive prose is seen in the description of the peewits' flight (lines 43-51). The key-word in this paragraph is the metaphorical *throb* (line 48). The beating of a heart excited by *anguish* and *protest* is reflected in the patterns of nature: the alternation of darkness and light ('the heralds wave like shadows in the bright air'); upward and downward movement ('Rising and falling'; 'They stoop suddenly to the ground, the lapwings, then in another throb of anguish and protest, they swing up again'); of giving and taking away ('. . . offering a glistening white breast to the sunlight, to deny it in black shadow'). The idea of the peewits' 'waving' is established in the rhythm created by a chain of present participles ('. . . crying, lamenting, fretting forever. Rising and falling and circling . . .'). Even a simple phrase like 'round and round' plays its part, because the repeated but contained sound, after the chain of weak-ended participles, suggests the difference between the fluttering and diving of the peewits and the pauses when they glide in circles. Similarly it is difficult to read the last sentence of this paragraph without feeling that the actual arrangement of words and phrases is telling us something over and beyond what they actually denote about the activity in the air: the dislocations ('They stoop suddenly to the ground, the lapwings, then . . .'), the repetitions ('glisten' and 'crying') and apparent breakdowns in syntax ('. . . to deny it in black shadow, then a glisten of green, and all the time . . .') seem designed to add another dimension to meaning.

Lawrence's prose is placed exuberantly at the service of sensation. In our imaginations we are made to see, hear, smell and feel the spring day and its activities. To take only one feature—movement— we find him completely in control: 'Birds called and flashed . . .' (lines 16–17); they *plunge* into the wood (line 18); the thrush *nestles* (line 34); the lapwings *stoop* into a dive and *swing up* again (lines 47, 48); the cock pheasant must 'spread himself on his streaming plumes and sail into the wood's security' (lines 54–5); the peewits *circle, turn, lift* and *full* (line 81); the swan 'swells onwards' (line 118).

With this accuracy of definition go those quite different touches of authority: the aphorism which we found growing out of the description of the peewits: 'They are like priests in their robes, more black than white, more grief than hope . . .' (lines 79–80); and the description of the lonely valley becomes an imaginative zeugma, 'full of sunshine and eternal forgetfulness' (line 113); while a conceit supplies a brilliant coda: 'The house was quiet and complacent; it was peopled by ghosts again, but the ghosts had only come to enjoy the warm place once more, carrying sunshine in their arms and scattering it through the dusk of gloomy rooms' (lines 137–41). If we can talk of a 'natural' actor who with little training can give memorable performances, here surely is a natural writer.

(2)

'I do so hate mysteries', Adela announced.
'We English do.'
'I dislike them not because I'm English, but from my own personal point of view', she corrected.
'I like mysteries but I rather dislike muddles', said Mrs   5
Moore.
'A mystery is a muddle.'

'Oh, do you think so, Mr Fielding?'

'A mystery is only a high-sounding term for a muddle. No
advantage in stirring it up, in either case. Aziz and I know well   10
that India's a muddle.'

'India's——Oh, what an alarming idea!'

'There'll be no muddle when you come to see me', said
Aziz, rather out of his depth. 'Mrs Moore and everyone—I
invite you all—oh, please.'   15

The old lady accepted: she still thought the young doctor
excessively nice; moreover, a new feeling, half languor, half
excitement, bade her turn down any fresh path. Miss Quested
accepted out of adventure. She also liked Aziz, and believed
that when she knew him better he would unlock his country   20
for her. His invitation gratified her, and she asked him for his
address.

Aziz thought of his bungalow with horror. It was a detest-
able shanty near a low bazaar. There was practically only
one room in it, and that infested with small black flies. 'Oh,   25
but we will talk of something else now', he exclaimed. 'I
wish I lived here. See this beautiful room! Let us admire
it together for a little. See those curves at the bottom of the
arches. What delicacy! It is the architecture of Question and
Answer. Mrs Moore, you are in India; I am not joking.'   30
The room inspired him. It was an audience hall built in the
eighteenth century for some high official, and though of wood
had reminded Fielding of the Loggia de' Lanzi at Florence.
Little rooms, now Europeanized, clung to it on either side,
but the central hall was unpapered and unglassed, and the air   35
of the garden poured in freely. One sat in public—on
exhibition, as it were—in full view of the gardeners who were
screaming at the birds and of the man who rented the tank for
the cultivation of water chestnut. Fielding let the mango trees
too—there was no knowing who might not come in—and   40
his servants sat on his steps night and day to discourage
thieves. Beautiful certainly, and the Englishman had not spoilt
it, whereas Aziz in an occidental moment would have hung
Maude Goodmans on the walls. Yet there was no doubt to
whom the room really belonged. . . .   45

'I am doing justice here. A poor widow who has been

robbed comes along and I give her fifty rupees, to another a
hundred, and so on and so on, I should like that.'

Mrs Moore smiled, thinking of the modern method as
exemplified in her son. 'Rupees don't last for ever, I'm afraid',   50
she said.

'Mine would. God would give me more when he saw I gave.
Always be giving, like the Nawab Bahadur. My father was the
same, that is why he died poor.' And pointing about the
room he peopled it with clerks and officials, all benevolent   55
because they lived long ago. 'So we would sit giving for
ever—on a carpet instead of chairs, that is the chief change
between now and then, but I think we would never punish
anyone.'

The ladies agreed.   60

'Poor criminal, give him another chance. It only makes a
man worse to go to prison and be corrupted.' His face grew
tender—the tenderness of one incapable of administration,
and unable to grasp that if the poor criminal is let off he
will again rob the poor widow. He was tender to everyone   65
except a few family enemies whom he did not consider
human: on these he desired revenge. He was even tender to
the English; he knew at the bottom of his heart that they could
not help being so cold and odd and circulating like an ice
stream through his land. 'We punish no one, no one,' he   70
repeated, and in the evening we will give a great banquet with a
nautch and lovely girls shall shine on every side of the tank
with fireworks in their hands, and all shall be feasting and
happiness until the next day, when there shall be justice as
before—fifty rupees, a hundred, a thousand—till peace comes.   75
Ah, why didn't we live in that time?—But are you admiring
Mr Fielding's house? Do look how the pillars are painted
blue, and the verandah's pavilions—what do you call them?—
that are above us inside are blue also. Look at the carving
on the pavilions. Think of the hours it took. Their little   80
roofs are curved to imitate bamboo. So pretty—and the
bamboos waving by the tank outside. Mrs Moore! Mrs Moore!'

'Well?' she said, laughing.

'You remember the water by our mosque? It comes down
and fills this tank—a skilful arrangement of the Emperors.   85

They stopped here going down into Bengal. They loved water.
Wherever they went they created fountains, gardens, hammams.
I was telling Mr Fielding I would give anything to serve
them.'

He was wrong about the water, which no Emperor, however   90
skilful, can cause to gravitate uphill; a depression of some
depth together with the whole of Chandrapore lay between the
mosque and Fielding's house. Ronny would have pulled him
up, Turton would have wanted to pull him up, but restrained
himself. Fielding did not even want to pull him up; he had   95
dulled his craving for verbal truth and cared chiefly for
truth of mood. As for Miss Quested, she accepted everything
Aziz said as true verbally. In her ignorance, she regarded him
as 'India', and never surmised that his outlook was limited
and his method inaccurate, and that no one is India.   100

He was now much excited, chattering away hard, and even
saying damn when he got mixed up in his sentences. He told
them of his profession, and of the operation he had witnessed
and performed, and he went into details that scared Mrs Moore,
though Miss Quested mistook them for proofs of his broad-   105
mindedness; she had heard such talk at home in advanced
academic circles, deliberately free. She supposed him to be
emancipated as well as reliable, and placed him on a pinnacle
which he could not retain. He was high enough for the
moment, to be sure, but not on any pinnacle. Wings bore him 110
up, and flagging would deposit him.

The arrival of Professor Godbole quieted him somewhat,
but it remained his afternoon. The Brahman, polite and
enigmatic did not impede his eloquence, and even applauded
it. He took his tea at a little distance from the outcasts, from 115
a low table placed slightly behind him, to which he stretched
back, and as it were encountered food by accident; all
feigned indifference to Professor Godbole's tea. He was
elderly and wizen with a grey moustache and grey-blue eyes,
and his complexion was as fair as a European's. He wore a   120
turban that looked like pale purple macaroni, coat, waistcoat,
dhoti, socks with clocks. The clocks matched the turban, and
his whole appearance suggested harmony—as if he had
reconciled the products of East and West, mental as well as

physical, and could never be discomposed. The ladies were 125
interested in him, and hoped that he would supplement Dr
Aziz by saying something about religion. But he only ate—ate
and ate, smiling, never letting his eyes catch sight of his hand.

E. M. FORSTER *A Passage to India*

In *A Passage to India*, E. M. Forster brings together characters of different
temperaments and backgrounds, members of a heterogeneous
society, to see if, by meeting and talking, they can find a way of
living in harmony with each other: 'Only connect', he tells them.
He is a skilful writer of dialogue and records the 'voices' of his
characters with great sensitivity.

In the conversations which have a central role in Forster's novels
there is always an extra voice—his own. It is never submerged
beneath those of his characters: his search for the total truth of a
situation precludes either that accidental identification which, in the
first extract, gave Lawrence and his hero one voice, or the deliberate
identification at which Virginia Woolf aims (3). The 'counterpoint'
which his method establishes—on the one hand dialogue, on the
other a commentary which complements and illuminates what is
said—is well illustrated here.

Fielding, who is committed to none of the racial or religious
groups whose uneasy relationship makes the India of the early
twentieth century a 'muddle', brings East and West, Mohammedan
and Hindu together at the tea-party in his summer-house. Mrs
Moore and Adela Quested are new arrivals who want to meet
Indians. Dr Aziz, a Mohammedan, has already had a friendly
encounter with Mrs Moore. Professor Godbole, a high-caste Hindu,
is a colleague of Fielding's. The occasion and the setting have a
significance of their own. A tea-party is a very English institution;
but Fielding's summer-house is a relic of the Mogul empire which
existed before the British conquest of India and it reminds Dr Aziz
of his Mohammedan forbears; Godbole introduces an alien note into
the familiar tea-party atmosphere by sitting apart from the others
at his own table since, as a Brahman, he must not eat with 'outcasts'.
This tea-party in an exotic setting is the frame which gives perspective
to what is said and done. Aziz's excited day-dreaming is unusual in
such a setting, and therefore fascinates the visitors; on the other

hand, his talk of operations at such a time seems to the older woman
a dangerous breach of properiety. Good manners forbid the
Englishwomen to stare, but they can only react with 'feigned indifference' to the sight of the Hindu eating his tea.

If Forster is successful, the result of his technique will be that we
learn a great deal about the characters from the way they talk. In the
role of Aziz he has to create the illusion of a man speaking fluently
and excitedly in a language whose nuances are lost on him. Forster
introduces us to a voice which is hasty, almost hectoring in its
uncertain beginnings; which struggles to minor climaxes of
rhetoric, drops as frequently into bathos and finally achieves
eloquence. Aziz's talk oscillates between extremes of poetry and
childish naivety. The evocative 'Mrs Moore you are in India'
(line 30) is let down by 'I am not joking' (line 30). At one moment
he is authoritative: 'It is the architecture of Question and Answer'
(lines 29–30); and at the next, boyish and confidential: 'I should like
that' (line 48). 'So we would sit giving for ever—' which promises
to be a graceful conclusion to his evocation of the vanished India,
plunges into the comic 'on a carpet instead of chairs, that is the chief
change between now and then . . .' (lines 57–8). His speech becomes
sentimental: 'Poor criminal, give him another chance' (line 61), and
takes on literary overtones '. . . lovely girls shall shine on every side
of the tank' (line 72); 'all shall be feasting and happiness' (lines 73–4).
But despite this uncertainty he rises at last to eloquence and we can
believe that we are listening to a man whose favourite pursuit is the
writing of poetry: 'Look at the carving on the partitions. Think of
the hours it took. Their little roofs are curved to imitate bamboo. So
pretty—and the bamboos waving by the tank outside. Mrs Moore!
Mrs Moore!' (lines 79–82). This is natural— the perception that the
architectural motif mirrors the reality outside is of a different order
from the more mannered: '. . . fifty rupees, a hundred, a thousand . . .'
(line 75) or 'Wherever they went they created fountains, gardens,
hammams' (line 87).

Forster is able to suggest different speech habits (reflecting
differences of temperament) in his English characters just as surely
as he established the alien ring in the diction and structure of Aziz's
speeches. Mrs Moore, Miss Quested and Fielding share the same
social background and, yet, even in the short space of the exchange
which begins this passage, we can hear their individual notes.

Miss Quested, strictly rational, enquiring, and a little priggish, naturally dislikes the irrational and mysterious. Her 'I do so hate' (line 1) is emphatic, but in a special way: 'do so hate' has a suggestion of idiosyncrasy and self-regard, which is not present in the simple 'hate'. Her second speech is a contradiction unsoftened by grace or humour. The 'not because . . . but from . . .' structure (lines 3-4) seems too literary and too sharply defined for this tea-party setting; we feel that the speaker is a little opinionated, self-conscious, pedantic. But the clumsy 'my own personal point of view', like 'do so hate', instead of giving emphasis, suggests the voice that overstates because it is unsure of itself.

Whereas Miss Quested's speech seems designed to convince others that she has a mind of her own, Fielding's reflects a quiet authority. In 'We English do' (line 2), 'A mystery is a muddle' (line 7), 'A mystery is only a high-sounding term for a muddle' (line 9), we hear the voice of a man whose experience allows him to generalize and clarify. The use of 'We' and the unpretentious 'high-sounding' suggests that Fielding understands himself; his own lack of illusions allows him to talk authoritatively about the illusions of others. Authority is felt also in the clipped, incisive 'No advantage in . . .' (lines 9-10) and the slightly patronizing assumption that Aziz will agree with him (as a good host he is trying to lead him back into the conversation): 'Aziz and I know well . . .' (line 10).

Mrs Moore's note is humorous and reflective. We feel that she knows more than she says. She has a natural self-confidence which Miss Quested lacks, and manages to imply that she has seen deeper into things than Fielding. It is Mrs Moore who distinguishes interestingly between mysteries and muddles. Her vague 'rather'—'I rather dislike muddles' (line 5)—seems designed to rob her statement of some of its force (in contrast to Miss Quested's tendency to overemphasize). She makes no overt attempt to contradict Fielding's dogmatic answer, but manages to imply disagreement with him. The use of Fielding's name, 'Oh, do you think so, Mr Fielding?' (line 8) conveys a certain irony; the rhetorical question might be transposed into a statement: 'That is only what Mr Fielding thinks'. There is also a touch of humour, almost mockery, in her reflective taking up of Fielding's dictum and dropping it again in pretended alarm: 'India's—— Oh, what an alarming idea!' (line 12).

Just as a theatrical 'set' is subjected to different kinds of lighting, which can produce noticeable changes of atmosphere, so the hard core of dialogue in Forster's novels is played on by his narrative. Having reproduced the physical properties of a situation (in this case, Fielding's room) and, in obedience to his inner ear, accurately recorded the voices of his characters, he proceeds to illuminate these given 'ingredients'. He can do so in three ways: by making us aware of his own feelings about the words and actions he is reporting; by interrupting his scene to bring in any outside information that has a bearing on it; and lastly by offering an interpretation of some of its aspects, which may seem insignificant in themselves but which to him are gateways to the ultimate truth which he is attempting to uncover.

The writer's feelings may be conveyed in a direct statement— 'His face grew tender—the tenderness of one incapable of administration' (lines 62–3). Sometimes they are perceived in a faint irony which exposes the weakness of a thought whilst apparently recording it impartially: 'And pointing about the room he peopled it with clerks and officials, all benevolent because they lived long ago' (lines 54–6). The image, 'like pale purple macaroni', makes Godbole and his turban comic. Forster's attitude is more often conveyed in the diction. We are advised to adopt a critical attitude towards Miss Quested in 'Adela announced' (line 1) and 'she corrected' (line 4); by rejecting the neutral 'she said', he implies his own dislike of her conversational manner. Aziz is subjected to the same kind of criticism; 'He was now much excited, chattering away hard, and even saying damn when he got mixed up in his sentences' (lines 101–2). The facetious 'much' (instead of 'very') the disdainful 'chattering' (instead of 'talking'), the 'even' designed to reflect Aziz's own ill-founded sense of daring, all betray a feeling of superiority towards him at this moment. Godbole's eating habits seem amusing when we are told that, with the table behind him, he 'as it were encountered food by accident' (line 117). But the ladies seem superficial in relation to the enigmatic Brahman when we learn that they 'hoped that he would supplement Dr Aziz by saying something about religion (lines 126–7).

The meeting of East and West in Fielding's summer house is accompanied by a commentary which clarifies the situation either by bringing in relevant information from outside, or by revealing the unspoken thoughts of the participants. This commentary, the second kind of narrative intervention, has a function similar to that of footnotes in a History, and brings to light the underlying attitudes which threaten the superficial harmony of the tea-party. We learn about the different reactions of Mrs Moore and Miss Quested to Aziz's account of his operations: the elderly Mrs Moore fears a breakdown of decorum; Miss Quested fails to realize that here she is confronted by a racial difference which has kept Aziz free from certain inhibitions, and she wrongly assumes that Aziz's frank speaking is the same deliberate rejecting of convention that it would have been amongst her 'advanced' English friends. We discover that the two women's motives for accepting Aziz's invitation are as different as their temperaments; and that Mrs Moore's smile (line 49) is provoked by her thoughts about the gap between Aziz's idea of justice and that of her magistrate-son. Another undercurrent is revealed in the digression in which Forster tells us how other English people would have reacted to Aziz's misrepresentation of fact—the water 'which no Emperor, however skilful, can cause to gravitate uphill' (lines 90–1). Fielding's sympathy with the oriental mind, revealed in his concern with 'truth of mood' (line 97), stands out against the supposed reactions of the new and the experienced officials, Ronny and Turton respectively. Aziz's action in giving an invitation and then retreating in confusion is illuminated by the picture we are given of his room, 'infested with small black flies' (line 25). We gain an insight which is withheld from Miss Quested as she bluntly asks him for his address. We gauge the extent of his desire to give pleasure by the fact of its having severed him momentarily from reality. His affection for Mrs Moore has as its foil his thoughts about the English in general: '. . . he knew at the bottom of his heart that they could not help being so cold and odd and circulating like an ice stream through his land' (lines 68–70). What at first seems to be an irrelevant statement (that the summer-house reminded Fielding of Florence) is designed to suggest that he is a man of wide interests, who has absorbed more than one culture, and is thus better equipped than the others to act as a bridge-maker.

So far, Forster has only presented us with facts from which we draw our own conclusions, helped, admittedly, by the tone of his writing ('Adela announced') and the arrangement of the ideas (the revelation of Aziz's vindictiveness, for example, coming just after he has assured his listeners that he would be a merciful judge). He goes further than merely selecting and presenting evidence, however.

There are certain conclusions at which we would not arrive even
when in possession of the facts. Forster is an authoritative writer:
after the constant appeals to our reasoning power, our ability to see
the relation of one fact to another and to make the right deductions,
he intervenes definitively and presents us not with the means to
truth, but the truth itself as he sees it. Sometimes these *ex cathedra*
utterances are in the form of flights of fancy, 'shots in the dark'. He
reaches the conclusion, for instance, in spite of all the evidence of
Aziz's bad, and Fielding's good taste, that the summer-house
'belongs' to Aziz: 'Beautiful certainly, and the Englishman had not
spoilt it, whereas Aziz in an occidental moment would have hung
Maude Goodmans on the walls. Yet there was no doubt to whom the
room really belonged' (lines 42–5).

Because Forster himself goes beyond reason and 'verbal truth' at
these moments, the voice of authority often has an undertone of
self-protective humour, and is sometimes embodied in images. The
conventional metaphor which makes Miss Quested place Aziz 'on a
pinnacle' is developed into an image which conveys, through
fantasy, a total impression of Aziz in relation to the tea-party:
'Wings bore him up, and flagging would deposit him' (lines 110–11).
Godbole's half-Indian, half-European clothes, especially the matching
socks and turban, which have been pointed out to us in a spirit of
comedy, are seized on as a symbol: 'The clocks matched the turban,
and his whole appearance suggested harmony—as if he had
reconciled the products of East and West, mental as well as physical,
and could never be discomposed' (lines 122–5). The voice of authority
is certainly muted, the 'as if' introducing almost deferentially the
flight into the irrational; but the events of the concluding chapters
of the novel, when Godbole comes into his own, show that Forster
is in this quiet way bringing to the surface one of the most prominent
strands of his theme.

Forster's 'voice' as a novelist is that of someone nearer to his
reader than to his characters. He appeals to intelligence rather than
emotion. As we have seen in this passage, he reveals character to the
reader, coolly and justly; but he does not follow that character into
the minutiae of experience in a way which would suggest identification with him. At the other extreme, there is no sustained irony to
fix character inescapably in an attitude or prejudice of his own.
When he reveals motivation he limits himself to the conscious

minds of his personages, as if to explore the irrational basis of
personality would undermine their dignity as members of organized
society. It is in symbols—sometimes chosen from the external
setting in which they find themselves—that he frees himself from the
limitations of the conscious, rational mind. It is most often in such
symbols, when they represent issues that reach beyond the individual
existence—like Godbole's turban and socks—that we encounter
strong feeling in E. M. Forster's work.

(3)

Certainly, Nancy had gone with them, since Minta Doyle had
asked it with her dumb look, holding out her hand, as Nancy
made off, after lunch, to her attic, to escape the horror of
family life. She had supposed she must go then. She did not
want to go. She did not want to be drawn into it all. For   5
as they walked along the road to the cliff Minta kept on taking
her hand. Then she would let it go. Then she would take
it again. What was it she wanted? Nancy asked herself. There
was something, of course, that people wanted; for when
Minta took her hand and held it, Nancy, reluctantly, saw the   10
whole world spread out beneath her, as if it were Constantinople seen through a mist, and then, however heavy-eyed one
might be, one must needs ask: 'Is that Santa Sofia?' 'Is that
the Golden Horn?' So Nancy asked, when Minta took her
hand: 'What is it that she wants? Is it that?' And what was   15
that? Here and there emerged from the mist (as Nancy looked
down upon life spread beneath her) a pinnacle, a dome;
prominent things, without names. But when Minta dropped her
hand, as she did when they ran down the hill-side, all that, the
dome, the pinnacle, whatever it was that had protruded   20
through the mist, sank down into it and disappeared.
   Minta, Andrew observed, was rather a good walker. She wore
more sensible clothes than most women. She wore very short
skirts and black knickerbockers. She would jump straight into
a stream and flounder across. He liked her rashness, but he   25
saw that it would not do—she would kill herself in some
idiotic way one of these days. She seemed to be afraid of
nothing except bulls. At the mere sight of a bull in a field

she would throw up her arms and fly screaming, which was the
very thing to enrage a bull of course. But she did not mind   30
owning up to it in the least; one must admit that. She knew
she was an awful coward about bulls, she said. She thought
she must have been tossed in her perambulator when she was
a baby. She didn't seem to mind what she said or did. Suddenly
now she pitched down on the edge of the cliff and began to   35
sing some song about

            Damn your eyes, damn your eyes.

They all had to join in and sing the chorus, and shout out
together:

            Damn your eyes, damn your eyes.   40

but it would be fatal to let the tide come in and cover up all
the good hunting-grounds before they got on to the beach.

   'Fatal', Paul agreed, springing up, and as they went slithering
down, he kept quoting the guide-book about 'these islands
being justly celebrated for their park-like prospects and the   45
extent and variety of their marine curiosities'. But it would
not do altogether, this shouting and damning your eyes,
Andrew felt, picking his way down the cliff, this clapping him
on the back, and calling him 'old fellow' and all that; it
would not altogether do. It was the worst of taking women   50
on walks. Once on the beach they separated, he going out on
to the Pope's Nose, taking his shoes off, and rolling his socks
in them and letting that couple look after themselves; Nancy
waded out to her own rocks and searched her own pools and let
that couple look after themselves. She crouched low down   55
and touched the smooth rubber-like sea anemones, who were
stuck like lumps of jelly to the side of the rock. Brooding,
she changed the pool into the sea, and made the minnows into
sharks and whales, and cast vast clouds over this tiny world
by holding her hand against the sun, and so brought darkness   60
and desolation, like God himself, to millions of ignorant and
innocent creatures, and then took her hand away suddenly and
let the sun stream down. Out on the pale criss-crossed sand,
high-stepping, fringed, gauntleted, stalked some fantastic
leviathan (she was still enlarging the pool), and slipped   65
into the vast fissures of the mountain-side. And then, letting her

eyes slide imperceptibly above the pool and rest on that
wavering line of sea and sky, on the tree trunks which the
smoke of steamers made waver upon the horizon, she became
with all that dower sweeping savagely in and inevitably   70
withdrawing, hypnotized, and the two senses of that vastness
and this tininess (the pool had diminished again) flowering
within it made her feel that she was bound hand and foot and
unable to move by the intensity of feelings which reduced her
own body, her own life, and the lives of all the people in the   75
world, for ever, to nothingness. So listening to the waves,
crouched over the pool, she brooded.

And Andrew shouted that the sea was coming in, so she leapt
splashing through the shallow waves on to the shore and ran up
the beach and was carried by her own impetuosity and her   80
desire for rapid movement right behind a rock and there oh
heavens! in each others arms were Paul and Minta! kissing
probably. She was outraged, indignant. She and Andrew put on
their shoes and stockings in dead silence without saying a thing
about it; indeed they were rather sharp with each other. She   85
might have called him when she saw the crayfish or whatever it
was, Andrew grumbled. However, they both felt, it's not our
fault. They had not wanted this horrid nuisance to happen. All
the same it irritated Andrew that Nancy should be a woman,
and Nancy that Andrew should be a man and they tied their   90
shoes very neatly and drew the bows rather tight.

VIRGINIA WOOLF, To the Lighthouse

In this episode from her novel, To the Lighthouse, Virginia Woolf
establishes the personalities of four characters who have previously
been little more than names. In the vaguely defined territory between
childhood and adult life are Andrew and Nancy Ramsay, still inclined
towards childhood, and Minta Doyle who is about to pass into the
adult world of love and marriage by accepting a proposal from Paul
Rayley.

Nancy is the most prominent of the four characters. In exploring
her inner life, Virginia Woolf uses a technique which allows her to
identify herself with the character she is creating. Sometimes Nancy's
'thoughts' are articulated as if in a speech: 'What is it that she

wants?' (line 15); sometimes the words she might have used if she
had voiced her thoughts are set down like reported speech: 'She did
not want to go' (lines 4–5). Words which a girl of Nancy's disposition
and background would have used are borrowed and used to colour
direct narrative: 'Certainly, Nancy had gone with them . . .' (line 1);
'There was something, of course . . .' (lines 8–9).—In these examples, we
can hear the over-emphatic language of children who are unsure of
themselves; in the 'one' of 'however heavy-eyed one might be, one
must needs ask' (lines 12–13), the personal masquerading shyly as the
impersonal. Virginia Woolf reveals Nancy's outlook by apparently
'adopting' as her own a phrase like 'the horror of family life' (lines 3–4).

Nancy is portrayed at the brink of an understanding of the
importance of sexual attraction in human relationships. She is both
intuitive and mistrustful of an intuition which threatens to sweep
away the landmarks of childhood. Her half-awareness and reluctance
to be aware are revealed by the vagueness of Virginia Woolf's style
when it reflects the girl's thoughts: 'She did not want to be drawn
into it all' (line 5); whereas a single conjunction, 'For' (line 5),
linking together apparently unconnected ideas, establishes her
intuitiveness: it is Minta's uncertain attitude towards her, expressed
in the taking and dropping of her hand, which gives her her first
awareness of being directly involved, on a footing of equality, with
adults. Her reluctance to respond is reflected in '. . . Minta kept on
taking her hand. Then she would let it go. Then she would take it
again'—flat and disjointed and so suggesting a child's troubled
reaction to signs which it is unwilling to translate. (Nancy has
turned herself back into an unintuitive child.)

Andrew's mental processes are quite different from his sister's. He
has no intuition: he observes and makes obvious deductions. He is
more rational and more responsive to what is happening round him.
Minta wears short skirts for walking: this is sensible. Minta is
impetuous: she may 'kill herself in some idiotic way' (lines 26–7).
While Nancy gropes towards new experiences in symbols or jumps
at them intuitively, Andrew's reflections are practical and the
products of reasoning: if Minta showed her fear of a bull by waving
her arms about she would enrage it all the more. Nancy's reluctant
intuition opened up Minta's personality for us. When Andrew thinks
of Minta we see her in spite of, rather than through, him. He fails to
recognize the element of flirtation in her admission that she is

frightened of bulls, and instead of realizing that she is playing on the protective instincts of her male companions, he judges the admission by his own, male, standards and admires her for admitting to a fear that he would have been ashamed of: 'But she did not mind owning up to it in the least; one must admit that' (lines 30–1); and her joke, 'She thought she must have been tossed in her perambulator when she was a baby' (lines 32–4) is transformed by him into a flat and humourless statement. Nancy and Andrew are united in their unwillingness to come to terms with the adult world which threatens to intrude on theirs. The thoughts of both brother and sister are recorded in the same words, as they go off to search the rock-pools and 'letting *that couple* look after themselves' (line 53). The young man, Paul, who is going to propose to Minta, is the intruder. His distance from them is marked by his perhaps satirical echoing of Andrew's 'fatal' (line 41)

Nancy's retreat from what Paul and Minta represent is a retreat into herself. Her mind interprets and therefore controls what she sees. According to her own vision, the rock pool into which she gazes can be an ocean, as she identifies herself with its smallest creatures, or a drop in an immense universe, when she relates it to the sea and the horizon. Both 'visions' offer an escape from the new experience that she is attempting to stave off. When she enlarges the pool, she also controls it: 'Like God himself' she can give or withhold sunlight by moving her hand. Paul and Minta become 'some fantastic leviathan' (lines 64–5) at the edge of her vision, as they walk across the beach and disappear behind their rock. When the pool is diminished in the scale of the universe, Paul and Minta with all other living creatures are reduced to insignificance; she has 'reduced her own body, her own life, and the lives of all the people in the world, for ever, to nothingness' (lines 74–6).

In her daydreams, Nancy can regain control over creatures and events at the very moment when in reality they are getting out of her control. Her complete absorption in the dream is illustrated by Andrew's having to warn her that she is about to be cut off by the incoming tide. Brooding gives way to a sudden burst of physical energy, and she is jolted back into reality when she finds Paul and Minta behind the rock. Virginia Woolf captures her distress first in echoes of Nancy's own language—'oh heavens!' (lines 81–2) and the terse, scornful, 'kissing probably' (lines 82–3)—and then in the deliberately extreme 'She was outraged, indignant' (line 83). The shock that she and Andrew have received is reflected in their silence, in Andrew's irritation over something irrelevant and trivial, in their attempt to cover up their confusion by concentrating on tying their shoes. Virginia Woolf borrows their own language once more: what has happened is a 'horrid nuisance' (line 88). The awareness of sex and the realization that they will have to move forward into an adult world is reflected in Andrew's irritation 'that Nancy should be a woman' (line 89) and Nancy's 'that Andrew should be a man' (line 90).

Virginia Woolf's method is to reproduce the moments at which experience is caught and reflected in the mind. Where Lawrence described the scene of the gamekeeper's funeral in minute detail and, while pretending to show his hero's reactions to it, actually showed his own, Virginia Woolf reveals the reactions of her characters by identifying herself with them, and leaves us to reconstruct those external events to which they respond. She does not appear in her own person, like E. M. Forster; she *tells* us nothing about her characters but tries to *show* us everything. In creating the mental world of Nancy and Andrew, she has left events to take care of themselves. It is only revealed afterwards that Paul has proposed to, and been accepted by, Minta. What would normally be the central point of a scene has been passed over. The reactions of the lovers are left to be guessed at. Minta is both the tomboy we see through Andrew's eyes and the woman he and Nancy find in Paul's arms. Her taking of Nancy's hand could represent both a reluctance to leave behind earlier, childhood loyalties and affections and, symbolically, a desire to lead Nancy into the adult world of lovers and marriage. Paul's preliminary nervousness might be assumed from his facetious quoting of the guide-book. To Nancy and Andrew they have already become 'that couple' who must be left to take care of themselves.

Virginia Woolf is able to handle situations as comprehensively and economically as this because her prose is both sensitive and adaptable. In the first paragraph of the extract we saw how, by transposing Nancy's thoughts into a kind of reported speech, she could associate herself with the girl at one moment and, the next, draw back as Nancy appears to speak these thoughts aloud. Perspective shifts with a single word or phrase. 'Certainly' (line 1) suggests a downrightness in Nancy, rather than the author; 'with her dumb look' (line 2) shows us that we are in the mind of the girl, to whom this look of Minta's is familiar and instantly recognizable. This knack of identification with the inner life of her characters can be traced to Virginia Woolf's prose rhythms as well as her choice of words. The structure of her sentences reflects the tempo at which people think and react to what is going on round them. Nancy's impetuousness, her embracing of ideas in a series of little rushes, is caught in the unusually jerky syntax of '. . . since Minta Doyle had asked it with her dumb look, holding out her hand, as Nancy made off, after lunch, to her attic, to escape the horror of family life' (lines 1–4). The strong feelings of a girl who knows her mind are caught in the quick sentences, heavily weighted with verbs and the repeated 'did not want' that follow: 'She had supposed she must go then. She did not want to go. She did not want to be drawn into it all' (lines 4–5). The verb 'to want' is allowed to dominate the paragraph, establishing the idea that people are vigorously reaching out for experience, or as vigorously attempting to reject it. But the forcefulness and certainty of 'want' is balanced against the uncertainty of 'it all' (line 5), 'something' (line 9), 'all that' (line 19), 'whatever it was' (line 20).

The nature of Andrew's grasp of experience is reflected in the structure of the second paragraph which consists largely of a series of statements about Minta Doyle. 'She wore more sensible clothes . . . She wore very short skirts . . . She would jump . . . She would kill herself . . . She seemed to be afraid of nothing . . . She did not mind . . . She knew . . . She thought . . . She didn't seem to mind . . .' (lines 22–34). This monotonous structure is designed to give prominence to statements of fact (and to verbs). While discovering that Andrew is unable to stop thoughts of Minta from running through his mind, we learn also about the nature of that mind: observant, in pursuit of facts; a young, stolid, rather humourless mind, already trying out, adult attitudes: 'he saw that it would not do' (lines 25–6), 'she would kill herself in some idiotic way' (lines 26–7), 'one must admit' (line 31), 'it would be fatal' (line 41).

Rhythm establishes the climax of the episode. The youthful impetuousness of Nancy's running through the waves and her sense of shock as her uncomfortable suspicions about Paul and Minta are substantiated, are reflected in the structure of the sentence: 'And Andrew shouted that the sea was coming in, so she leapt splashing through the shallow waves on to the shore and ran up the beach and was carried by her own impetuosity and her desire for rapid movement right behind a rock and there oh heavens! in each others arms were Paul and Minta! kissing probably' (*lines 78–83*). The excitement of the sudden burst of activity is caught in the breathlessness of the loosely-strung syntax with its conjunctions, 'and' and, 'so'; 'right behind' reflects the emphatic, exaggerated manner in which the girl herself would have spoken about the incident: and the sentence dies like a spent firework after its two little explosions, the first, the girlish 'oh heavens!', as she catches sight of the lovers, and the second as her mind registers the fact that they are embracing.

Virginia Woolf's sensitiveness to mood is reflected in the comparatively prim words interspersed in the description of the aftermath: 'indeed' (*line 85*) and 'However' (*line 87*), which suggest the stilted, formal language of people trying to recover their balance. The parallelism of the last sentence and its emphatic adverbs, 'very' and 'rather' have the same effect: 'All the same it irritated Andrew that Nancy should be a woman, and Nancy that Andrew should be a man and they tied their shoes very neatly and drew the bows rather tight' (*lines 88–91*).

In her attempt to reproduce the inner world of reverie and symbol-making, Virginia Woolf embraces the irrational and bizarre. These are the commonplaces of the interior life. Nancy's unconscious attempt to make sense of the confused feelings to which the unvoiced request in Minta's hand gives rise, ends in the birth of a symbol: 'Constantinople seen through a mist' (*lines 11–12*). It would be irrelevant to ask if Virginia Woolf is aware of the incongruous, and consequently humorous, element in the daydream. Humour belongs to the rational mind: here she is exploring it at a level where the reason is impinged on by the subconscious. She follows her character closely into the details of the dream: '. . . however heavy-eyed one might be, one must needs ask: "Is that Santa Sofia?" "Is that the Golden Horn?" ' (*lines 11–12*)—the fact that there is no rational connection between such details and what is happening on Nancy's walk to the beach with Minta makes no difference: Nancy's half-intuition of what is going on in Minta's mind—what she 'wants'—is pinned down in symbol like a butterfly. At such moments, it is the 'real', exterior world which becomes the 'less real' quantity. The events of the walk are relegated to a subordinate clause: 'But when Minta dropped her hand, *as she did when they ran down the hillside*, all that, the dome, the pinnacle, whatever it was that had protruded through the mist, sank down into it and disappeared' (lines 18–21). (Similarly, the fact that they climb down the cliff becomes only a modifying phrase in a description of Andrew's thoughts: 'But it would not do altogether, this shouting and damning your eyes, Andrew felt, picking his way down the cliff, this clapping him on the back, and calling him "old fellow" and all that; it would not altogether do' (lines 46–50).)

We follow Nancy straight into the dream perspective she creates as she broods over the pool: '. . . she changed the pool into the sea, and made the minnows into sharks and whales . . .' (lines 58–9). The tone is the same as when we were told that Andrew took his shoes off: no barrier separates the two realities. The only difference is that now we are closely identified, once more, with Nancy's thoughts; it is she who thinks in terms of 'like God himself' (line 61), and of 'ignorant and innocent creatures' (lines 61–2); the adjectives which describe Paul and Minta as they stroll across the beach—in the girl's daydream, a leviathan—'high-stepping, fringed, gauntleted . . . fantastic' (line 64)—are Nancy's, not the narrator's. The lines of smoke rising from the horizon are not like tree-trunks: they have actually become them in Nancy's mind.

The distortion of the girl's vision as, crouching over the pool and keeping it in focus, she sees, magnified and out of focus, the advancing and retreating waves, is matched by a distortion of syntax: '. . . she became with all that dower sweeping savagely in and inevitably withdrawing, hypnotized . . .' (lines 69–71). Her excitement is captured in the diction. The scene has lost its factual properties: it is not a wave but a 'dower' that sweeps into her line of vision. (Here it was necessary to reject the concrete for the abstract because the idea that what is coming towards her is only a wave, has already been rejected by Nancy. For a moment, as she plays tricks with her vision and so with reality, exterior things have lost not only their normal scale but also the labels which the mind usually gives them; she can only think of a wave in terms of an unidentifiable 'gift' which Nature happens to offer her at that moment.) The movement of the waves on a summer day is 'savage' not in reality but in her mind. Her realization of the vastness of the universe is registered in the expanding structure, the repetitions, the pause, 'for ever', before the climax, of '. . . which reduced her own body, her own life, and the lives of all the people in the world, for ever, to nothingness' (lines 74–6).

PASSAGES FOR ANALYSIS ONE

Earliest fears; the mystery of death; the vividly recalled sights and sounds and smells of childhood; the different scale of one's surroundings when surveyed from a height of three feet instead of five or six; the passages that follow have a good deal of subject matter in common. Differences in texture and tone will reflect the differing sensibilities of the writers' audiences as well as the temperament of the writers themselves—*David Copperfield* (A) was published in 1850 and Laurie Lee's *Cider with Rosie* in 1959. It should also be remembered that *David Copperfield* is a novel with autobiographical elements, while *Cider with Rosie* is a series of autobiographical short stories.

A

Looking back, as I was saying, into the blank of my infancy, the first objects I can remember as standing out by themselves from a confusion of things, are my mother and Peggotty. What else do I remember? Let me see.

There comes out of the cloud, our house—not new to me,   5
but quite familiar, in its earliest remembrance. On the ground-floor is Peggotty's kitchen, opening into a back yard; with a pigeon-house on a pole, in the centre, without any pigeons in it; a great dog-kennel in a corner, without any dog; and a quantity of fowls that look terribly tall to me, walking   10
about in a menacing and ferocious manner. There is one cock who gets upon a post to crow, and seems to take particular notice of me as I look at him through the kitchen window,

who makes me shiver, he is so fierce. Of the geese outside the
side-gate who come waddling after me with their long necks   15
stretched out when I go that way, I dream at night; as a man
environed by wild beasts might dream of lions.

Here is a long passage—what an enormous perspective I
make of it!—leading from Peggotty's kitchen to the front
door. A dark store-room opens out of it, and that is a place to   20
be run past at night; for I don't know what may be among
those tubs and jars and old tea-chests, when there is nobody
in there with a dimly-burning light, letting a mouldy air
come out at the door, in which there is the smell of soap, pickles,
pepper, candles, and coffee, all at one whiff. Then there are the   25
two parlours; the parlour in which we sit of an evening, my
mother and I and Peggotty—for Peggotty is quite our
companion, when her work is done and we are alone—and
the best parlour where we sit on a Sunday; grandly, but not
so comfortably. There is something of a doleful air about that   30
room to me, for Peggotty has told me—I don't know when,
but apparently ages ago—about my father's funeral, and the
company having their black cloaks put on. One Sunday night
my mother reads to Peggotty and me in there, how Lazarus
was raised up from the dead. And I am so frightened that   35
they are afterwards obliged to take me out of bed, and show
me the quiet churchyard out of the bedroom window, with
the dead all lying in their graves at rest, below the solemn
moon.

There is nothing half so green that I know anywhere, as the
grass of that churchyard; nothing half so shady as its trees;   40
nothing half so quiet as its tombstones. The sheep are feeding
there, when I kneel up, early in the morning, in my little bed
in a closet within my mother's room, to look out at it; and I
see the red light shining on the sun-dial, and think within
myself, 'Is the sun-dial glad, I wonder, that it can tell the time   45
again?'

CHARLES DICKENS, David Copperfield

1   What mood has the writer tried to evoke? What methods has
he used for this purpose, and with what success?

2   Here is a long passage—what an enormous perspective I make
of it!—leading from Peggotty's kitchen to the front door.

Discuss the attitude towards a) the reader, and b) himself as a
child, revealed by the writer in this sentence.

3   Consider the effectiveness of the imagery in which he represents
the act of remembering (lines 1–6).

4   Consider the relationship between intention and syntax in the
sentences:

There is one cock . . . he is so fierce. (lines 11–14)
Of the geese . . . of lions. (lines 14–17)

5   Consider the following words and phrases in their contexts.
Do you think they were well chosen?

ferocious (line 11), to be (lines 21–2), of (line 26), grandly (line 29),
something of (line 30), And (line 35), I wonder (line 45).

B

Radiating from that house, with its crumbling walls, its
thumps and shadows, its fancied foxes under the floor, I
moved along paths that lengthened inch by inch with my
mounting strength of days. From stone to stone in the
trackless yard I sent forth my acorn shell of senses, moving   5
through unfathomable oceans like a South Sea savage island-
hopping across the Pacific. Antennae of eyes and nose and
grubbing fingers captured a new tuft of grass, a fern, a slug,
the skull of a bird, a grotto of bright snails. Through the long
summer ages of those first few days I enlarged my world and   10
mapped in my mind its secure havens, its dust-deserts and
puddles, its peaks of dirt and flag-flying bushes. Returning
too, dry-throated, over and over again, to its several well-
prodded horrors: the bird's gaping bones in its cage of old
sticks; the black flies in the corner, slimy dead; dry rags of   15

snakes; and the crowded, rotting silent-roaring city of a cat's grub-captured carcass.

Once seen, these relics passed within the frontiers of the known lands, to be remembered with a buzzing in the ears, to be revisited when the stomach was strong. They were the first tangible victims of that destroying force whose job I knew went on both night and day, though I could never catch him at it. Nevertheless I was grateful for them. Though they haunted my eyes and stuck in my dreams, they reduced for me the first infinite possibilities of horror. They chastened the imagination with the proof of a limited frightfulness.

From the harbour mouth of the scullery door I learned the rocks and reefs and the channels where safety lay. I discovered the physical pyramid of the cottage, its stores and labyrinths, its centres of magic, and of the green, sprouting island-garden upon which it stood. My Mother and sisters sailed past me like galleons in their busy dresses, and I learned the smells and sounds which followed in their wakes, the surge of breath, air of carbolic, song and grumble, and smashing of crockery.

LAURIE LEE, *Cider With Rosie*

1   What is the writer trying to achieve in this passage?

2   Do you agree with the opinion that the first paragraph is overburdened with imagery?

3   Consider the following words and phrases in their contexts. Do you think they were well chosen?

> Radiating (line 1), fancied (line 2), trackless (line 5), antennae (line 7), dry-throated (line 13), tangible (line 21), limited (line 26), pyramid (line 29).

4   Consider the relationship between diction and subject matter.

5   'Returning too, dry-throated, over and over again, to its several well-prodded horrors: the bird's gaping bones in its cage of old sticks; the black flies in the corner, slimy dead; dry rags of snakes; and the crowded, rotting silent-roaring city of a cat's grub-captured carcass.'

> What contribution does rhythm make to the effect of this sentence?

COMPARATIVE STUDY

1   Consider the kind of relationship with the reader which each author presupposes.

2   Consider the element of humour in each passage. Which do you find the more successful in this respect? Which has the wider range of feeling?

3   Examine the parts played by imagery (i.e. metaphors and similes) and rhythm in helping to reproduce the experience of being a child.

4   Has the handling of the imaginative material in *A* been affected at all by the necessity (in the second chapter of a novel) to create the setting for a story?—Would you be inclined to read on?

5   What qualities in *B* would encourage you to continue reading?

TWO

Perhaps the most successful actors of farce are those who can hurl
themselves into its sequence of disasters with as much solemnity as if
they were playing *Hamlet*. The following passages are both taken from
tall stories told with straight faces. Both writers make fun of some of
the intellectual preoccupations of their times: Thomas Love Peacock
(in *Headlong Hall* (A) published in 1837) laughs at scientific and
philosophical speculation and at the cult of sensibility reflected in
such diverse interests as the drama and landscape gardening; while
the Thurber passage (B) (from *My Life and Hard Times*, published in
1933) seems to pay a certain tongue-in-cheek homage to the
achievements of psychiatry.

A

Mr Milestone superintended the proceedings. The rock was
excavated, the powder introduced, the apertures strongly
blockaded with fragments of stone: a long train was laid to
a spot which Mr Milestone fixed on as sufficiently remote
from the possibility of harm: the Squire seized the poker,   5
and, after flourishing it in the air with a degree of dexterity
which induced the rest of the party to leave him in solitary
possession of an extensive circumference, applied the end of
it to the train; and the rapidly-communicated ignition ran
hissing along the surface of the soil.   10
    At this critical moment, Mr Cranium and Mr Panscope
appeared at the top of the tower, which, unseeing and unseen,
they had ascended on the opposite side to that where the Squire
and Mr Milestone were conducting their operations. Their
sudden appearance a little dismayed the Squire, who, however, 15

comforted himself with the reflection that the tower was
perfectly safe, or at least was intended to be so, and that his
friends were in no probable danger but of a knock on the head
from a flying fragment of stone.

The succession of these thoughts in the mind of the Squire   20
was commensurate in rapidity to the progress of the ignition,
which having reached its extremity, the explosion took place,
and the shattered rock was hurled into the air in the midst of
fire and smoke.

Mr Milestone had properly calculated the force of the   25
explosion; for the tower remained untouched: but the
Squire, in his consolatory reflections, had omitted the com-
sideration of the influence of sudden fear, which had so
violent an effect on Mr Cranium, who was just commencing
a speech concerning the very fine prospect from the top of the 30
tower, that cutting short the thread of his observations, he
bounded, under the elastic influence of terror, several feet into
the air. His ascent being unluckily a little out of the perpen-
dicular, he descended with a proportionate curve from the apex
of his projection, and alighted not on the wall of the tower,   35
but in an ivy-bush by its side, which, giving way beneath him,
transferred him to a tuft of hazel at its base, which after
upholding him an instant, consigned him to the boughs of an
ash that had rooted itself in a fissure about half-way down the
rock, which finally transmitted him to the waters below.   40

Squire Headlong anxiously watched the tower as the smoke
which at first enveloped it rolled away; but when this shadowy
curtain was withdrawn, and Mr Panscope was discovered, *solus*,
in a tragical attitude, his apprehensions became boundless, and
he concluded that the unlucky collision of a flying fragment of 45
rock had indeed emancipated the spirit of the craniologist
from its terrestrial bondage.

THOMAS LOVE PEACOCK, *Headlong Hall*

1   Give a brief and purely factual account of the events in the
passage.

2   Attempt to distinguish between the parts played by events,
characterization and narrative technique.

3   What relationship is the writer of this passage trying to establish with the reader?

4   Is the diction of the fourth paragraph in keeping with this intention?

5   Comment on
    a) the diction of paragraph 3
    b) the imagery of lines 37–40
    c) the structure of lines 26–33 ('but the Squire . . . into the air.')

B

But I am straying from the remarkable incidents that took place during the night that the bed fell on father. By midnight we were all in bed. The layout of the rooms and the disposition of their occupants is important to an understanding of what later occurred. In the front room upstairs (just under father's attic   5 bedroom) were my mother and my brother Herman, who sometimes sang in his sleep, usually 'Marching Through Georgia' or 'Onward, Christian Soldiers'. Briggs Beall and myself were in a room adjoining this one. My brother Roy was in a room across the hall from ours. Our bull terrier, Rex, slept   10 in the hall.

My bed was an army cot, one of those affairs which are made wide enough to sleep on comfortably only by putting up, flat with the middle section, the two sides which ordinarily hang down like the sideboards of a drop-leaf table. When these   15 sides are up, it is perilous to roll too far toward the edge, for then the cot is likely to tip completely over, bringing the whole bed down on top of one, with a tremendous banging crash. This, in fact, is precisely what happened, about two o'clock in the morning. (It was my mother who, in recalling   20 the scene later, first referred to it as 'the night the bed fell on your father'.)

Always a deep sleeper, slow to arouse (I had lied to Briggs),
I was at first unconscious of what had happened when the iron
cot rolled me on to the floor and toppled over on me. It left me   25
still warmly bundled up and unhurt, for the bed rested above
me like a canopy. Hence I did not wake up, only reached the
edge of consciousness and went back. The racket, however,
instantly awakened my mother, in the next room, who came
to the immediate conclusion that her worst dread was   30
realized: the big wooden bed upstairs had fallen on father.
She therefore screamed, 'Let's go to your poor father!' It was
this shout, rather than the noise of my cot falling, that
awakened Herman, in the same room with her. He thought
that mother had become, for no apparent reason, hysterical.   35
'You're all right, Mamma!' he shouted, trying to calm her.
They exchanged shout for shout for perhaps ten seconds:
'Let's go to your poor father!' and 'You're all right!' That
woke up Briggs. By this time I was conscious of what was
going on, in a vague way, but did not yet realize that I was   40
under my bed instead of on it. Briggs, awakening in the midst
of loud shouts of fear and apprehension, came to the quick
conclusion that he was suffocating and that we were all trying
to 'bring him out'. With a low moan, he grasped the glass of
camphor at the head of his bed and instead of sniffing it   45
poured it over himself. The room reeked of camphor. 'Ugf,
ahfg', choked Briggs, like a drowning man, for he had almost
succeeded in stopping his breath under the deluge of pungent
spirits. He leaped out of bed and groped toward the open
window, but he came up against one that was closed. With his   50
hand, he beat out the glass, and I could hear it crash and tinkle
on the alleyway below. It was at this juncture that I, in trying
to get up, had the uncanny sensation of feeling my bed above
me! Foggy with sleep, I now suspected, in my turn, that the
whole uproar was being made in a frantic endeavour to   55
extricate me from what must be an unheard-of and perilous
situation. 'Get me out of this!' I bawled. 'Get me out!' I think
I had the nightmarish belief that I was entombed in a mine.
'Gugh', gasped Briggs, floundering in his camphor.

By this time my mother, still shouting, pursued by Herman,   60
still shouting, was trying to open the door to the attic, in order

to go up and get my father's body out of the wreckage. The
door was stuck, however, and wouldn't yield. Her frantic pulls
on it only added to the general banging and confusion. Roy
and the dog were now up, the one shouting questions, the   65
other barking.

Father, farthest away and the soundest sleeper of all, had by
this time been awakened by the battering on the attic door. He
decided that the house was on fire. 'I'm coming, I'm coming!'
he wailed in a slow, sleepy voice—it took him many minutes   70
to regain full consciousness. My mother, still believing he was
caught under the bed, detected in his 'I'm coming!' the
mournful resigned note of one who is preparing to meet his
Maker. 'He's dying!' she shouted.

JAMES THURBER, *My Life and Hard Times*

1   Give a brief and purely factual account of the events of the
passage.

2   Attempt to distinguish between the parts played by events and
narrative technique.

3   What relationship is the writer trying to establish with the
reader?

4   'This passage owes its success to its restraint.' Discuss.

5   Comment on the use of descriptive detail in the following
extracts:

         My bed was an army cot . . .
                . . . a tremendous banging crash. (lines 12–19)

         The room reeked of camphor . . .
                . . . on the alleyway below. (lines 46–52)

6   Describe the effect of the following sentences:
         Our bull terrier, Rex, slept in the hall. (lines 10–11)

         Roy and the dog were now up, the one shouting questions,
the other barking. (lines 64–6)

COMPARATIVE STUDY

'The humour is the same, but the techniques are different.' Discuss.

THREE

The great achievement of *Emma* is to give us an imaginative experience of a small community in which the social relationships of the various members are sharply defined. Jane Austen has done so despite the apparent handicap of having, as narrator, adopted a viewpoint very close to that of her heroine, a girl of twenty-one whose judgments are frequently wrong. In this extract from Chapter 4—an account of Emma's new friendship with Harriet Smith, an illegitimate girl of seventeen who is a 'parlour-boarder' at Mrs Goddard's school—we learn as much about Emma's character-deficiencies (and possible excuses for them) as about Harriet; and beyond the immediate situation we catch a momentary, but clear, glimpse of Mr Robert Martin—clearer perhaps than Harriet's or Emma's view of him, for the humour of this passage springs from the fact that, while Emma perceives more acutely than Harriet, the reader is constantly invited to perceive with much greater clarity than either Harriet or the self-assured young heroine.

Harriet Smith's intimacy at Hartfield was soon a settled thing. Quick and decided in her ways, Emma lost no time in inviting, encouraging, and telling her to come very often; and as their acquaintance increased, so did their satisfaction in each other. As a walking companion, Emma had very early foreseen how   5
useful she might find her. In that respect Mrs Weston's loss had been important. Her father never went beyond the shrubbery, where two divisions of the ground sufficed him for his long walk, or his short, as the year varied; and since Mrs Weston's marriage her exercise had been too much confined.   10
She had ventured once alone to Randall's but it was not pleasant; and a Harriet Smith, therefore, one whom she could summon at any time to a walk, would be a valuable addition to her privileges. But in every respect, as she saw more of her, she approved her, and was confirmed in all her kind designs.   15

Harriet certainly was not clever, but she had a sweet, docile, grateful disposition, was totally free from conceit, and only desiring to be guided by any one she looked up to. Her early attachment to herself was very amiable; and her inclination for good company, and power of appreciating what was elegant and clever, shewed that there was no want of taste, though strength of understanding must not be expected. Altogether she was quite convinced of Harriet Smith's being exactly the young friend she wanted—exactly the something which her home required. Such a friend as Mrs Weston was out of the question. Two such could never be granted. Two such she did not want. It was quite a different sort of thing, a sentiment distinct and independent. Mrs Weston was the object of a regard which had its basis in gratitude and esteem. Harriet would be loved as one to whom she could be useful. For Mrs Weston there was nothing to be done; for Harriet everything.

Her first attempts at usefulness were in an endeavour to find out who were the parents; but Harriet could not tell. She was ready to tell everything in her power, but on this subject questions were vain. Emma was obliged to fancy what she liked; but she could never believe that in the same situation she should not have discovered the truth. Harriet had no penetration. She had been satisfied to hear and believe just what Mrs Goddard chose to tell her; and looked no farther.

Mrs Goddard, and the teachers, and the girls, and the affairs of the school in general, formed naturally a great part of the conversation—and but for her acquaintance with the Martins of Abbey Mill Farm, it must have been the whole. But the Martins occupied her thoughts a good deal; she had spent two very happy months with them, and now loved to talk of the pleasures of her visit, and describe the many comforts and wonders of the place. Emma encouraged her talkativeness, amused by such a picture of another set of beings, and enjoying the youthful simplicity which could speak with so much exultation of Mrs Martin's having 'two parlours, two very good parlours, indeed; one of them quite as large as Mrs Goddard's drawing-room; and of her having an upper maid who had lived five-and-twenty years with her; and of their having eight cows, two of them Alderneys, and one a little

Welch cow, a very pretty little Welch cow indeed; and of Mrs   55
Martin's saying, as she was so fond of it, it should be called her
cow; and of their having a very handsome summer-house in
their garden, where some day next year they were all to drink
tea; a very handsome summer-house, large enough to hold a
dozen people'.   60

For some time she was amused, without thinking beyond
the immediate cause; but as she came to understand the
family better, other feelings arose. She had taken up a wrong
idea, fancying it was a mother and daughter, a son and a son's
wife, who all lived together; but when it appeared that the Mr   65
Martin, who bore a part in the narrative, and was always
mentioned with approbation for his great good-nature in
doing something or other, was a single man—that there was
no young Mrs Martin, no wife in the case—she did suspect
danger to her poor little friend from all this hospitality and   70
kindness, and that, if she were not taken care of, she might be
required to sink herself for ever.

With this inspiriting notion, her questions increased in
number and meaning; and she particularly led Harriet to talk
more of Mr Martin, and there was evidently no dislike to it.   75
Harriet was very ready to speak of the share he had had in their
moonlight walks and merry evening games; and dwelt a good
deal upon his being so very good-humoured and obliging.
'He had gone three miles round one day in order to bring her
some walnuts, because she had said how fond she was of them,   80
and in everything else he was so very obliging. He had his
shepherd's son into the parlour one night on purpose to sing
to her. She was very fond of singing. He could sing a little
himself. She believed he was very clever, and understood everything. He had a very fine flock, and while she was with them,   85
he had been bid more for his wool than anybody in the
country. She believed everybody spoke well of him. His
mother and sisters were very fond of him. Mrs Martin had told
her one day (and there was a blush as she said it) that it was
impossible for anybody to be a better son, and therefore she was   90
sure, whenever he married, he would make a good husband.
Not that she wanted him to marry. She was in no hurry at
all.'

'Well done, Mrs Martin!' thought Emma. 'You know what you are about.'

'And when she had come away, Mrs Martin was so very kind   95
as to send Mrs Goddard a beautiful goose—the finest goose Mrs Goddard had ever seen. Mrs Goddard had dressed it on a Sunday, and asked all the three teachers, Miss Nash, and Miss Prince, and Miss Richardson to sup with her.'

'Mr Martin, I suppose, is not a man of information beyond   100
the line of his own business? He does not read?'

'Oh yes!—that is, no—I do not know—but I believe he has read a good deal—but not what you would think anything of. He reads the *Agricultural Reports*, and some other books that lay in one of the window seats—but he reads all them to himself.   105
But sometimes of an evening, before we went to cards, he would read something aloud out of the *Elegant Extracts*, very entertaining. And I know he has read the *Vicar of Wakefield*. He never read the *Romance of the Forest*, nor the *Children of the Abbey*. He had never heard of such books before I mentioned them, but he is   110
determined to get them now as soon as ever he can.'

The next question was—

'What sort of looking man is Mr Martin?'

'Oh! not handsome—not at all handsome. I thought him very plain at first, but I do not think him so plain now. One   115
does not, you know, after a time. But did you never see him? He is in Highbury every now and then, and he is sure to ride through every week in his way to Kingston. He has passed you very often.'

'That may be, and I may have seen him fifty times, but   120
without having any idea of his name. A young farmer, whether on horseback or on foot, is the very last sort of person to raise my curiosity. The yeomanry are precisely the order of people with whom I feel I can have nothing to do. A degree or two lower, and a creditable appearance might interest me; I   125
might hope to be useful to their families in some way or other. But a farmer can need none of my help, and is, therefore, in one sense, as much above my notice as in every other he is below it.'

JANE AUSTEN, *Emma*

1   What is Jane Austen's opinion of a) her heroine, b) Harriet, and c) Mr Martin?

2   Consider the ambiguities in Emma's relationship with Harriet. How are these suggested in the first two paragraphs?

3   What part does this extract play in indicating Emma's social position in Hartfield?

4   How much do we learn about Emma's growing influence over Harriet from the exchange in lines 100–11?

5   What intention are we meant to perceive behind Emma's questions in lines 100–1?

6   What are Jane Austen's feelings about the Martins? Does she succeed in indicating them without abandoning her position as a narrator closely identified with her heroine?

7   How does she contrive to show us Mr Martin's feelings about Harriet? To what extent is she helped in this by the limitations with which she has already 'endowed' Harriet?

8   Consider the contribution made by prose rhythm to the establishing of Emma's personality in the second half of paragraph 2.

9   'One of the achievements of this passage is that the writer has been able to create the impression of a personage listening as well as talking.' Do you agree? If so, how has this effect been suggested?

10   Do we hear Harriet's voice in the indirect, as well as the direct, speech?

11   To what extent does our feeling about Harriet depend on the structure of lines 47–60?

12   In spite of the narrator's apparent identification with Emma, we are continually informed about the realities of the situation. Consider the role of the following extracts in communicating this information, and give the name of the principle stylistic device involved:

    a) . . . her inclination for good company, and power of appreciating what was elegant and clever, shewed that there was no want of taste . . . (lines 19–21)

    b) Emma encouraged her talkativeness, amused by such a picture of another set of beings, and enjoying the youthful simplicity which could speak with so much exultation of . . . (lines 47–50)

c) . . . she did suspect danger to her poor little friend from all this hospitality and kindness . . . (lines 69–70)

13   Consider the significance of the following words and phrases:

useful (line 6), summon (line 13), grateful (line 17), obliged (line 35), in the case (line 69), inspiriting (line 73), meaning (line 74).

FOUR

Two middle-class Victorians are dissected by writers who reacted against the society and traditions in which they had been brought up. Much of Samuel Butler's savage indignation in *The Way of All Flesh*—a novel which has been described as an act of patricide and matricide—is directed against his parents, 'Theobald and Christina Pontifex'. John Galsworthy writes with much less bitterness and in his portrait of James Forsyte, in *A Man of Property*, criticism of the man fades into criticism of the social mores that have formed him.

A

By nature reserved, if he could have found someone to cook his dinner for him, he would rather have lived in a desert island than not. In his heart of hearts he held with Pope that 'the greatest nuisance to mankind is man' or words to that effect—only that women, with the exception perhaps of   5
Christina, were worse. Yet for all this, when visitors called he put a better face on it than any one who was behind the scenes would have expected.

He was quick too at introducing the names of any literary celebrities whom he had met at his father's house, and soon   10
established an all-round reputation which satisfied even Christina herself.

Who so *integer vitae sclerisque purus*,[1] it was asked, as Mr Pontifex of Battersby? Who so fit to be consulted if any difficulty about parish management should arise? Who such a happy mixture   15
of the sincere uninquiring Christian and of the man of the world? For so people actually called him. They said he was

[1]   upright in his ways and free from vice

such an admirable man of business. Certainly if he had said he
would pay a sum of money at a certain time, the money would
be forthcoming on the appointed day, and this is saying a good   20
deal for any man. His constitutional timidity rendered him
incapable of an attempt to overreach when there was the
remotest chance of opposition or publicity, and his correct
bearing and somewhat stern expression were a great protection
to him against being overreached. He never talked of money,   25
and invariably changed the subject whenever money was
introduced. His expression of unutterable horror at all kinds
of meanness was a sufficient guarantee that he was not mean
himself. Besides, he had no business transactions save of the
most ordinary butcher's book and baker's book description.   30
His tastes—if he had any—were, as we have seen, simple; he
had £900 a year and a house; the neighbourhood was cheap,
and for some time he had no children to be a drag upon him.
Who was not to be envied, and if envied why then respected,
if Theobald was not enviable?   35

   Yet I imagine that Christina was on the whole happier than
her husband. She had not to go and visit sick parishioners, and
the management of her house and the keeping of her accounts
afforded as much occupation as she desired. Her principal duty
was, as she well said, to her husband—to love him, honour   40
him, and keep him in a good temper. To do her justice, she
fulfilled this duty to the uttermost of her power. It would have
been better perhaps if she had not so frequently assured her
husband that he was the best and wisest of mankind, for no one
in his little world ever dreamed of telling him anything else,   45
and it was not long before he ceased to have any doubt upon
the matter. As for his temper, which had become very violent
at times, she took care to humour it on the slightest sign of an
approaching outbreak. She had early found that this was much
the easiest plan. The thunder was seldom for herself. Long   50
before her marriage even she had studied his little ways, and
knew how to add fuel to the fire as long as the fire seemed to
want it, and then to damp it judiciously down, making as little
smoke as possible.

SAMUEL BUTLER, The Way of All Flesh

1   Consider the effect on the tone of the first two paragraphs of:
         rather . . . than not (lines 2–3), perhaps (line 5), behind the
         scenes (line 7), even (line 11).

2   Attempt to outline the character of the narrator. What is his
attitude towards a) his parents (Theobald and Christina Pontifex),
and b) Pontifex's parishioners?

3   Try to account stylistically for the differences in tone between
a) lines 27–33 ('His expression of unutterable horror . . . to be a drag
upon him') and b) lines 47–54 ('As for his temper . . . making as
little smoke as possible.')

4   'A failure to come to terms with his subject, which is reflected
in the uncertainties of the style.'

    'A satirical attack which is all the more effective for having
avoided the strait-jacket of sustained irony.'

    Which of these opinions do you consider nearer the truth?

5   Consider the effect in their contexts of the following:
         uninquiring (line 16), when there was the remotest chance of
         opposition or publicity (lines 22–3), to love him, honour him
         and keep him in a good temper (lines 40–1), to do her justice
         (line 41).

B

Than James Forsyte, notwithstanding all his 'Jonah-isms', there
was no saner man (if the leading symptom of sanity, as we are
told, is self-preservation, though without doubt Timothy went
too far) in all this London, of which he owned so much, and
loved with such a dumb love, as the centre of his opportunities.   5
He had the marvellous instinctive sanity of the middle class. In
him—more than in Jolyon, with his masterful will and his
moments of tenderness and philosophy—more than in Swithin,
the martyr to crankiness—Nicholas, the sufferer from
ability—and Roger, the victim of enterprise—beat the true   10
pulse of compromise; of all the brothers he was least remark-

able in mind and person, and for that reason more likely to
live for ever.

To James, more than to any of the others, was 'the family'
significant and dear. There had always been something   15
primitive and cosy in his attitude towards life; he loved the
family hearth, he loved gossip, and he loved grumbling. All his
decisions were formed of a cream which he skimmed off the
family mind; and through that family, off the minds of
thousands of other families of similar fibre. Year after year,   20
week after week, he went to Timothy's, and in his brother's
front drawing-room—his legs twisted, his long white whiskers
framing his clean-shaven mouth—would sit watching the
family pot simmer, the cream rising to the top; and he would
go away sheltered, refreshed, comforted, with an indefinable   25
sense of comfort.

Beneath the adamant of his self-preserving instinct there was
much real softness in James; a visit to Timothy's was like an
hour spent in the lap of a mother; and the deep craving he
himself had for the protection of the family wing reacted in   30
turn on his feelings towards his own children; it was a
nightmare to him to think of them exposed to the treatment of
the world, in money, health, or reputation. When his old
friend John Street's son volunteered for special service, he shook
his head querulously, and wondered what John Street was   35
about to allow it: and when young Street was assagaied, he
took it so much to heart that he made a point of calling
everywhere with the special object of saying, 'He knew how
it would be—he'd no patience with them!'

When his son-in-law Dartie had that financial crisis, due to   40
speculation in Oil Shares, James made himself ill worrying over
it; the knell of all prosperity seemed to have sounded. It took
him three months and a visit to Baden-Baden to get better;
there was something terrible in the idea that but for his,
James's, money Dartie's name might have appeared in the   45
Bankruptcy List.

Composed of a physiological mixture so sound that if he
had ear-ache he thought he was dying, he regarded the
occasional ailments of his wife and children as in the nature of
personal grievances, special interventions of Providence for the   50

purpose of destroying his peace of mind; but he did not believe at all in the ailments of people outside his own immediate family, affirming them in every case to be due to neglected liver.

His universal comment was: 'What can they expect? I have   55
it myself if I'm not careful!'

JOHN GALSWORTHY, *A Man of Property*

1   What attitude towards the middle classes is implied in the first paragraph?

2   Instinctive (line 6), instinct (line 27), primitive (line 16): is the use of these words justified by the contents of the passage?

3   Comment on the use of the verb 'love' in lines 4, 16 and 17.

4   Examine the parts played by a) imagery and b) anecdote in establishing James Forsyte's character.

5   Analyse the relationship between intention and structure in the first paragraph.

COMPARATIVE STUDY

1   Which writer do you consider to have been the more successful in blending together external facts and his own opinion of the character he is portraying?

2   A commonly held view of characterization in the novel is that the writer should be objective about the personages he describes. (Jane Austen, for example, has been criticized for too obviously liking Fanny Price and disliking Mrs Norris in *Mansfield Park*.) Have these writers been objective? Has either gained, or lost, by failing to be so?

3   There are elements of humour in both passages—but very different kinds of humour. What does the difference tell us about the personalities of the writers and their attitudes towards the men they are describing?

4   Which writer has been the more successful in engaging your feelings?

FIVE

The contributions that can be made by metaphor, diction and rhythm when an exotic atmosphere has to be evoked would be seen if we attempted to reduce the following descriptions to their bare, strictly topographical, outlines. But stylistic virtuosity should never be an end in itself; and one of the questions raised by the extracts is, At what point does truth end and self-consciousness begin?

A

The slight quiver agitating the whole fabric of the ship was more perceptible in the silent river, shaded and still like a forest path. The Sofala, gliding with an even motion, had passed beyond the coast-belt of mud and mangrove-swamps. The shores rose higher, in firm sloping banks, and the forest of 5 big trees came down to the brink. Where the earth had been crumbled by the floods it showed a steep brown cut, denuding a mass of roots intertwined as if wrestling underground; and in the air, the interlaced boughs, bound and loaded with creepers, carried on the struggle for life, mingled their foliage 10 in one solid wall of leaves, with here and there the shape of an enormous dark pillar soaring, or a ragged opening, as if torn by the flight of a cannon-ball, disclosing the impenetrable gloom within, the secular inviolable shade of the virgin forest. The thump of the engines reverbrated regularly like the strokes 15 of a metronome beating the measure of the vast silence, the shadow of the western wall had fallen across the river, and the smoke pouring backwards from the funnel eddied down behind the ship, spread a thin dusky veil over the sombre water, which, checked by the flood-tide, seemed to lie stagnant in the whole   20 straight length of the reaches.

JOSEPH CONRAD, The End of the Tether

1   Break down this scene into a list of its component parts.

2   Consider the effect that the imagery of lines 8–10 has on the rest of the passage.

3   What aspects of the scene has the writer tried to emphasize? Does this emphasis improve the description or impede the artistic illusion that we are actually seeing what the writer describes?

4   Consider the following words and phrases in their contexts. Do you think they were well chosen?

> like a forest path (lines 2–3), crumbled (line 7), wall (line 11), inviolable (line 14), eddied (line 18).

5   Consider the purpose and effectiveness of the conceit in lines 15–16.

6   Explore the relationship between sound, rhythm and sense in the following sentences:

> The slight quiver . . . forest path. (lines 1–3)
> The Sofala . . . mangrove-swamps. (lines 3–4)
> The thump . . . the reaches. (lines 15–21)

B

The evening was very still and quiet, rather as if it had caught its own breath at the beauty and brilliance of the night that was marching down on it out of the East like a goddess with jewels of fire. An immense full moon had swung itself clear over the dark fringe of the jungle bound, like a ceremonial   5 fringe of ostrich plumes designed for an ancient barbaric ritual, to the dark brow of the land ahead. In that responsive

and plastic tropical air the moon seemed magnified to twice
its normal size and to be quicksilver wet and dripping with
its own light. To the north of the jungle and all along its heavy   10
feathered fringes the sea rolled and unrolled its silver and gold
cloak on to the white and sparkling sand, as lightly and
deftly as a fine old far-eastern merchant unrolling bales of his
choicest silk. The ancient, patient swish of it all was constantly
in Lawrence's ears. But far out on the horizon, the sea too went   15
dark, seemed shrunk into a close defensive ring, in face of the
thunder and lightning hurled against it by curled, curved and
jagged peaks of cloud which stood revealed on the uttermost
edge by the intermittent electric glow imperative in purple
and sullen in gold.   20

LAURENS VAN DER POST, *A Bar of Shadow*

1   Break down this scene into a list of its component parts.

2   Consider the purpose and effectiveness of the conceit in lines
1–2.

3   Analyse the following similes with regard to accuracy and
appropriateness:

> like a ceremonial fringe or ostrich plumes (*lines* 5–6)
> as a fine old far-eastern merchant unrolling bales of his
> choicest silk (*lines* 13–14)

4   'Spoilt by an obtrusive anthropomorphism.' Is this a fair
comment?

5   Consider the use of sound effects in the last two sentences.

6   Consider the following words and phrases in their contexts.
Do you think they were well chosen?

> rather (line 1), swung (line 4), barbaric (line 6), deftly (line
> 13), curled, curved and jagged peaks (*lines* 17–18), imperative (line
> 19)

COMPARATIVE STUDY

1   Do these passages, individually, prove the usefulness or the
dangers of personification in descriptive writing?

2   Which description gives you the keener sense of seeing what the writer saw?

3   Intrinsic properties of a scene brought to the surface: extrinsic properties added to provide excitement.

Are these techniques equally valuable? Is their use illustrated here?

4   Make a comparative study of the two passages, paying special attention to rhythm and diction.

SIX

Charles Dickens and Henry James both reveal themselves to be sceptical about professional philanthropists, and illustrate the dangers to which they are exposed when their public activities intrude upon their private lives. The passage from Bleak House (A) is entirely satirical: in Henry James's description of Miss Birdseye satire blends with a gentler comedy and sense of pathos—though it might have been from Dickens that James learnt the effectiveness of apparently glaringly incongruous comparisons.

Miss Birdseye is seen partly through the eyes of Basil Ransom. The narrative structure of Bleak House demands that Mrs Jellyby should be seen entirely through the eyes of her young visitor, the gentle Esther Summerson—and whether or not Dickens has succeeded in maintaining this impersonation is a question to be explored.

A

We passed several more children on the way up, whom it was difficult to avoid treading on in the dark; and as we came into Mrs Jellyby's presence, one of the poor little things fell downstairs a whole flight (as it sounded to me), with a great noise. 5

Mrs Jellyby, whose face reflected none of the uneasiness which we could not help showing in our own faces, as the dear child's head recorded its passage with a bump on every stair—Richard afterwards said he counted seven, besides one for the landing—received us with perfect 10 equanimity. She was a pretty, very diminutive, plump

woman, of from forty to fifty, with handsome eyes, though they
had a curious habit of seeming to look a long way off. As if
—I am quoting Richard again—they could see nothing
nearer than Africa!   15
'I am very glad indeed', said Mrs Jellyby, in an agreeable
voice, 'to have the pleasure of receiving you. I have a great
respect for Mr Jarndyce; and no one in whom he is interested
can be an object of indifference to me.'

We expressed our acknowledgments, and sat down behind   20
the door where there was a lame invalid of a sofa. Mrs Jellyby
had very good hair, but was too much occupied with her
African duties to brush it. The shawl in which she had been
loosely muffled, dropped on to her chair when she advanced to
us; and as she turned to resume her seat, we could not help   25
noticing that her dress didn't nearly meet up the back, and that
the open space was railed across with a lattice-work of stay-
lace—like a summer-house.

The room, which was strewn with papers and nearly filled
by a great writing-table covered with similar litter, was, I   30
must say, not only very untidy, but very dirty. We were
obliged to take notice of that with our sense of sight, even
while, with our sense of hearing, we followed the poor child
who had tumbled downstairs: I think into the back kitchen,
where somebody seemed to stifle him.   35

'You find me, my dears,' said Mrs Jellyby, snuffing the two
great office candles in tin candlesticks which made the room
taste strongly of hot tallow (the fire had gone out, and there
was nothing in the grate but ashes, a bundle of wood, and a
poker), 'you find me, my dears, as usual, very busy; but that   40
you will excuse. The African project at present employs my
whole time. It involves me in correspondence with public
bodies, and with private individuals anxious for the welfare
of their species all over the country. I am happy to say it is
advancing. We hope by this time next year to have from a   45
hundred and fifty to two hundred healthy families cultivating
coffee and educating the natives of Borrioboola-Gha, on the
left bank of the Niger.

CHARLES DICKENS, Bleak House

1   What is Dickens's chief criticism of Mrs Jellyby?

2   Distinguish between the writer's and the narrator's attitudes towards Mrs Jellyby. The narrator is a young woman. Has the writer been successful in his use of this *persona*?

3   Examine the incident of the child falling downstairs. Is it relevant to the theme of the passage? Has the writer done anything to diminish the reader's concern for the child?

4   How much do we learn about Mrs Jellyby from a) her appearance, b) her surroundings, c) her conversation?

5   Consider the importance in this passage of incongruity, in a) ideas, and b) imagery.

6   Analyse the structure of the sentence
     'You find me . . . that you will excuse.' (lines 36–41)
     Do you agree with the opinion that it is clumsy?

B

She had a sad, soft, pale face, which (and it was the effect of her whole head) looked as if it had been soaked, blurred, and made vague by exposure to some slow dissolvent. The long practice of philanthropy had not given accent to her features; it had rubbed out their transitions, their meaning. The waves of   5
sympathy, of enthusiasm, had wrought upon them in the same way in which the waves of time finally modify the surfaces of old marble busts, gradually washing away their sharpness, their details. In her large countenance her dim little smile scarcely showed. It was a mere sketch of a smile, a kind of   10
instalment, or payment on account; it seemed to say that she would smile more if she had time, but that you could see, without this, that she was gentle and easy to beguile.
    She always dressed in the same way: she wore a loose black jacket, with deep pockets, which were stuffed with papers,   15
memoranda of a voluminous correspondence; and from

beneath her jacket depended a short stuff dress. The brevity of
this simple garment was the one device by which Miss
Birdseye managed to suggest that she was a woman of business,
that she wished to be free for action. She belonged to the   20
Short-Skirts League, as a matter of course; for she belonged to
any and every league that had been founded for almost any
purpose whatever. This did not prevent her being a confused,
entangled, inconsequent, discursive old woman, whose charity
began at home and ended nowhere, whose credulity kept pace   25
with it, and who knew less about her fellow-creatures, if
possible, after fifty years of humanity zeal, than on the day
she had gone into the field to testify against the iniquity of
most arrangements. Basil Ransom knew very little about such
a life as hers, but she seemed to him a revelation of a class, and   30
a multitude of socialistic figures, of names and episodes that he
had heard of, grouped themselves behind her. She looked as if
she had spent her life on platforms, in audiences, in conventions, in phalansteries, in seances; in her faded face there was
a kind of reflection of ugly lecture-lamps; with its habit of an   35
upward angle, it seemed turned toward a public speaker, with
an effort of respiration in the thick air in which social reforms
are usually discussed. She talked continually, in a voice of
which the spring seemed broken, like that of an over-worked
bell-wire.   40

HENRY JAMES, *The Bostonians*

1   What effect did Miss Birdseye's philanthropy have on her
character? What paradox is hinted at in lines 3-5 and 10-13?

2   What are Henry James's feelings about Miss Birdseye?

3   Analyse the first two sentences, paying special attention to the
interplay of facts, images and the writer's interpretation of his
character's appearance. Can they be defended from the criticism that
they are unnecessarily repetitive? What is the mood of these
sentences? How is that mood generated?

4   Consider the relationship between syntax and intention in the
sentence

This did not prevent her . . . most arrangements. (lines 23-9)

5   Is the final simile appropriate? Consider the relationship
between it and

   a) the description of Miss Birdseye's smile (lines 10–13) and
b) the 'marble busts' comparison (lines 6–9).

COMPARATIVE STUDY

1   Consider the contrasting techniques of character-portrayal
illustrated here.

2   Consider the relationship between imagery and satire in the
passages.

3   Explore the usefulness of simile and metaphor as satirical
weapons.

4   'Where Dickens will sacrifice verisimilitude for a single
comic stroke, James will forego opportunities for comedy in order
to obtain a closer insight into a character.' Examine the two passages
in the light of this comment.

SEVEN

The hero of Graham Greene's *The Power and the Glory* is a priest on the run in a Mexican state where the Catholic Church has been proscribed. He faces execution if his identity is discovered. He is alone, and in this episode has come to a ranch in the hope of finding help and food. But the ranch has been abandoned.

The passage gives an example of how a writer can convey a character's inner experience while appearing to concentrate on the external events in which he is involved.

He turned moodily again to stare out at the clearing, and there was the Indian woman creeping back—towards the hut where he had sheltered. He called out to her sharply and again she fled, shambling, towards the forest. Her clumsy progress reminded him of a bird feigning a broken wing. . . . He made no movement to follow her, and before she reached the trees she stopped and watched him; he began to move slowly back towards the other hut. Once he turned: she was following him at a distance, keeping her eyes on him. Again he was reminded of something animal or bird-like, full of anxiety. He walked on, aiming directly at the hut—far away beyond it the lightning stabbed down, but you could hardly hear the thunder: the sky was clearing overhead and the moon came out. Suddenly he heard an odd artificial cry, and turning he saw the woman making back towards the forest—then she stumbled, flung up her arms and fell to the ground—like the bird offering herself.

He felt quite certain now that something valuable was in the hut, perhaps hidden among the maize, and he paid her no attention, going in. Now that the lightning had moved on, he couldn't see—he felt across the floor until he reached the pile of maize. Outside the padding footsteps came nearer. He began to feel all over it—perhaps food was hidden there—and the dry crackle of the leaves was added to the drip of water and the

5

10

15

20

cautious footsteps, like the faint noises of people busy about
their private businesses. Then he put his hand on a face.   25

He couldn't be frightened any more by a thing like that—
it was something human he had his fingers on. They moved
down the body: it was a child's who lay completely quiet under
his hand. In the doorway the moonlight showed the woman's
face indistinctly: she was probably convulsed with anxiety,   30
but you couldn't tell. He thought—I must get this into the
open where I can see . . .

It was a male child—perhaps three years old: a withered
bullet head with a mop of black hair: unconscious—but not
dead: he could feel the faintest movement in the breast. He   35
thought of disease again until he took out his hand and found
that the child was wet with blood, not sweat. Horror and disgust
touched him—violence everywhere: was there no end to
violence? He said to the woman sharply: 'What happened?' It
was as if man in all this state had been left to man.   40

The woman knelt two or three feet away, watching his hands.
She knew a little Spanish, because she replied: 'Americano.'
The child wore a kind of brown one-piece smock: he lifted it
up to the neck: he had been shot in three places. Life was going
out of him all the time: there was nothing—really—to be   45
done, but one had to try. . . . He said 'Water' to the woman,
'Water', but she didn't seem to understand, squatting there,
watching him. It was a mistake one easily made, to think that
just because the eyes expressed nothing there was no grief.
When he touched the child he could see her move on her   50
haunches—she was ready to attack him with her teeth if the
child so much as moaned.

He began to speak slowly and gently (he couldn't tell how
much she understood): 'We must have water. To wash him.
You needn't be afraid of me. I will do him no harm.' He took   55
off his shirt and began to tear it into strips—it was hopelessly
insanitary, but what else was there to do? except pray, of
course, but one didn't pray for life, this life. He repeated again:
'Water'. The woman seemed to understand—she gazed
hopelessly round at where the rain stood in pools—that was   60
all there was. Well, he thought, the earth's as clean as any vessel
would have been. He soaked a piece of his shirt and leant over

the child: he could hear the woman slide closer along the
ground—a menacing approach. He tried to reassure her again:
'You needn't be afraid of me. I am a priest.'   65
    The word 'priest' she understood: she leant forward and
grabbed at the hand which held the wet scrap of shirt and
kissed it. At that moment, while her lips were on his hand,
the child's face wrinkled, the eyes opened and glared at them,
the tiny body shook with a kind of fury of pain; they watched   70
the eyeballs roll up and suddenly become fixed, like marbles
in a solitaire-board, yellow and ugly with death. The woman
let go his hand and scrambled to a pool of water, cupping her
fingers for it. The priest said, 'We don't need that any more',
standing up with his hands full of wet shirt. The woman   75
opened her fingers and let the water fall. She said 'Father'
imploringly, and he wearily went down on his knees and
began to pray.
    He could feel no meaning any longer in prayers like these—
the Host was different: to lay that between a dying man's lips   80
was to lay God. That was a fact—something you could touch,
but this was no more than pious aspiration. Why should
Anyone listen to his prayers? Sin was a constriction which
prevented their escape: he could feel his prayers like undigested
food heavy in his body, unable to escape.   85
    When he had finished he lifted up the body and carried it
back into the hut like a piece of furniture—it seemed a waste of
time to have taken it out, like a chair you carry out into the
garden and back again because the grass is wet. The woman
followed him meekly—she didn't seem to want to touch the   90
body, just watched him put it back in the dark upon the maize.

GRAHAM GREENE, The Power and the Glory

1   What part do the similes in the first paragraph play in a)
giving accurate pictures of the events described, and b) intensifying
one aspect of the priest's situation? How have they been prepared for
in the first two sentences? Is the view of human life that they suggest
borne out elsewhere in the passage?

2   Are the hero's reactions convincingly those of a priest?

3   Examine the means used to suggest that, for this man, feeling is a luxury that has had to be abandoned.

4   What viewpoint has the narrator adopted?

5   'He felt quite certain now that something valuable was in the hut' (lines 17–18). Explore the way in which this idea is developed to suggest first the physical and then the spiritual realities of this situation.

6   Analyse the rhythm of events and the paragraphing of lines 21–7. Explore the way in which the reader is drawn into the protagonist's experience.

7   Consider the interplay of intention and rhythm in the sentence 'It was a male child . . . (lines 33–5).

8   Consider the narrative technique used in lines 37–40 and lines 46–9. What is gained by presenting material in this way?

9   Analyse the interplay of actions (especially the order in which things happen), diction and similes in the paragraph beginning 'The word "priest" ' (lines 66–78). What comment on the nature of life is Greene making here?

10   Could the digestion metaphor in lines 83–5 be defended from the criticism that it was inappropriate?

11   Consider the relationship between the 'chair' simile (line 88) and the diction of the same paragraph.

EIGHT

The passages that follow will probably attract attention in the first place for the vivid descriptions of nature they contain. These descriptions are used as settings for very different human situations: Yeobright, in Thomas Hardy's *Return of the Native* (A) is a young intellectual who has recently made an unfortunate marriage and who is going blind. The hero-narrator in the D. H. Lawrence passage (B) is describing the part that friendship has played in his growing-up, and this extract is full of youthful delight in a bombardment of sensations. But the impression of solitariness in A and the enthusiastic perception of harmonies in B both depend to a large extent on their authors' ability to engage our sympathy through appeals to the senses.

A

This man from Paris was now so disguised by his leather accoutrements, and by the goggles he was obliged to wear over his eyes, that his closest friend might have passed by without recognising him. He was a brown spot in the midst of an expanse of olive-green gorse, and nothing more. Though frequently depressed in spirit when not actually at work, owing to thoughts of Eustacia's position and his mother's estrangement, when in the full swing of labour he was cheerfully disposed and calm.

His daily life was of a curious microscopic sort, his whole world being limited to a circuit of a few feet from his person. His familiars were creeping and winged things, and

5

10

they seemed to enrol him in their band. Bees hummed around
his ears with an intimate air, and tugged at the heath and
furze-flowers at his side in such numbers as to weigh them   15
down to the sod. The strange amber-coloured butterflies which
Egdon produced, and which were never seen elsewhere,
quivered in the breath of his lips, alighted upon his bowed
back, and sported with the glittering point of his hook as he
flourished it up and down. Tribes of emerald-green grass-   20
hoppers leaped over his feet, falling awkwardly on their backs,
heads, or hips, like unskilful acrobats, as chance might rule; or
engaged themselves in noisy flirtations under the fern-fronds
with silent ones of homely hue. Huge flies, ignorant of
larders and wire-netting, and quite in a savage state, buzzed   25
about him without knowing that he was a man. In and out of the
fern-dells snakes glided in their most brilliant blue and
yellow guise, it being the season immediately following the
shedding of their old skins, when their colours are brightest.
Litters of young rabbits came out from their forms to sun   30
themselves upon hillocks, the hot beams blazing through the
delicate tissue of each thin-fleshed ear, and firing it to a blood-
red transparency in which the veins could be seen. None of
them feared him.

The monotony of his occupation soothed him, and was in   35
itself a pleasure. A forced limitation of effort offered a
justification of homely courses to an unambitious man, whose
conscience would hardly have allowed him to remain in such
obscurity while his powers were unimpeded. Hence Yeobright
sometimes sang to himself, and when obliged to accompany   40
Humphrey in search of brambles for faggot-bonds he would
amuse his companion with sketches of Parisian life and
character, and so while away the time.

On one of these warm afternoons Eustacia walked out alone
in the direction of Yeobright's place of work. He was busily   45
chopping away at the furze, a long row of faggots which
stretched downward from his position representing the labour
of the day. He did not observe her approach, and she stood close
to him, and heard his undercurrent of song. It shocked her. To
see him there, a poor afflicted man, earning money by the   50
sweat of his brow, had at first moved her to tears; but to hear

him sing and not at all rebel against an occupation which, however satisfactory to himself, was degrading to her, as an educated lady-wife, wounded her through.

THOMAS HARDY, *The Return of the Native*

1   How does the writer try to convey the experience of a man threatened with blindness?

2   Define the tone of the following sentences:

    a) Though frequently depressed . . . and calm. (lines 5–9)
    b) Huge flies . . . was a man. (lines 24–6)
    c) To see him there . . . wounded her through. (lines 49–54)

3   What are the writer's feelings about the situation of Yeobright and his wife, Eustacia? How does he communicate them to us?

4   Consider the effect of the following words and phrases:

    This man from Paris (line 1)
    and nothing more (line 5)
    as chance might rule (line 22)

5   Can the use of personification in paragraph 2 be justified?

B

I was born in September, and love it best of all the months. There is no heat, no hurry, no thirst and weariness in corn harvest as there is in the hay. If the season is late, as is usual with us, then mid-September sees the corn still standing on stook. The mornings come slowly. The earth is like a woman   5 married and fading; she does not leap up with a laugh for the first fresh kiss of dawn, but slowly, quietly, unexpectantly lies watching the waking of each new day. The blue mist, like memory in the eyes of a neglected wife, never goes from the wooded hill, and only at noon creeps from the near hedges.   10 There is no bird to put a song in the throat of morning; only

the crow's voice speaks during the day. Perhaps there is the regular breathing hush of the scythe—even the fretful jar of the mowing machine. But next day, in the morning, all is still again. The lying corn is wet, and when you have bound it and   15
lift the heavy sheaf to make the stook, the tresses of oats wreathe round each other and droop mournfully.

As I worked with my friend through the still mornings we talked endlessly. I would give him the gist of what I knew of chemistry, and botany, and psychology. Day after day I told   20
him what the professors had told me; of life, of sex and its origins; of Schopenhauer and William James. We had been friends for years, and he was accustomed to my talk. But this autumn fruited the first crop of intimacy between us. I talked a great deal of poetry to him, and of rudimentary metaphysics.   25
He was very good stuff. He had hardly a single dogma, save that of pleasing himself. Religion was nothing to him. So he heard all I had to say with an open mind, and understood the drift of things very rapidly, and quickly made these ideas part of himself.   30

We tramped down to dinner with only the clinging warmth of the sunshine for a coat. In this still, enfolding weather a quiet companionship is very grateful. Autumn creeps through everything. The little damsons in the pudding taste of September, and are fragrant with memory. The voices of those   35
at table are softer and more reminiscent than at haytime.

Afternoon is all warm and golden. Oat sheaves are lighter; they whisper to each other as they freely embrace. The long, stout stubble tinkles as the foot brushes over it; the scent of the straw is sweet. When the poor, bleached sheaves are lifted out   40
of the hedge, a spray of nodding wild raspberries is disclosed, with belated berries ready to drop; among the damp grass lush blackberries may be discovered. Then one notices that the last bell hangs from the ragged spire of fox-glove. The talk is of people, but not of life; where the plains are wide, and one is   45
not lapped in a soft valley, like an apple that falls in a secluded orchard. The mist steals over the face of the warm afternoon. The tying-up is all finished, and it only remains to rear up the fallen bundles into shocks. The sun sinks into a golden glow in the west. The gold turns to red, the red darkens, like a fire   50

burning low, the sun disappears behind the bank of milky mist,
purple like the pale bloom on blue plums, and we put on our
coats and go home.

D. H. LAWRENCE, *The White Peacock*

1   Try to reconstruct the September day described here, and
explore the development of the idea of autumnal dampness.

2   ' . . . and love it best of all the months'. Consider the part
played by the idea of love in this passage.

3   'An effective use of contrasts'. Do you agree?

4   Has the 'pathetic fallacy' been used successfully?

5   Define the tone of this writing. To what extent is it influenced
by the writer's sensory alertness?

6   Consider the effect of the following:

> But this autumn fruited the first crop of intimacy between
> us. (lines 23–4)
> Autumn creeps through everything. (lines 33–4)

COMPARATIVE STUDY

1   Try to establish the degrees of success with which these writers
have created a link between people and nature.

2   One of the passages is from a first novel. Which?

3   'The pessimism of A can be traced to the clear definition that is
given to the relationship between Yeobright and his surroundings:
the gaiety and confidence of B are the products of a reckless use of
the pathetic fallacy.' Discuss.

4   Would it be reasonable or not to suggest that one of these
views of life was more valid than the other?

NINE

In the following passages, the heroines of George Eliot's *Middlemarch*
(A) and E. M. Forster's *A Passage to India* (B) find themselves in alien
surroundings, without the necessary key to understanding and
enjoying them. Both are at turning points in their lives. By describing their characters' reactions—or failure to react—to places,
George Eliot and E. M. Forster are trying to suggest to us what is
happening in the less conscious regions of their minds.

A

*Dorothea Brooke has recently married an elderly and unsympathetic scholar with
the intention of helping him complete his life's work. She spends a lonely honeymoon
in Rome, where her husband's research has taken them.*

To those who have looked at Rome with the quickening
power of a knowledge which breathes a growing soul into
all historic shapes, and traces out the suppressed transitions
which unite all contrasts, Rome may still be the spiritual
centre and interpreter of the world. But let them conceive one   5
more historical contrast; the gigantic broken revelations of that
Imperial and Papal city thrust abruptly on the notions of a girl
who had been brought up in English and Swiss Puritanism, fed
on meagre Protestant histories and on art chiefly of the hand-
screen sort; a girl whose ardent nature turned all her small   10
allowance of knowledge into principles, fusing her actions into
their mould, and whose quick emotions gave the most abstract

things the quality of a pleasure or a pain; a girl who had lately
become a wife, and from the enthusiastic acceptance of untried
duty found herself plunged in tumultuous preoccupation with   15
her personal lot. The weight of unintelligible Rome might lie
easily on bright nymphs to whom it formed a background for
the brilliant picnic of Anglo-foreign society; but Dorothea had
no such defence against deep impressions. Ruins and basilicas,
palaces and colossi, set in the midst of a sordid present, where   20
all that was living and warm-blooded seemed sunk in the deep
degeneracy of a superstition divorced from reverence; and
dimmer but yet eager Titanic life gazing and struggling on walls
and ceiling; the long vistas of white forms whose marble eyes
seemed to hold the monotonous light of an alien world: all   25
this vast wreck of ambitious ideals, sensuous and spiritual,
mixed confusedly with the signs of breathing forgetfulness and
degradation, at first jarred her as with an electric shock, and
then urged themselves on her with that ache belonging to a
glut of confused ideas which check the flow of emotion. Forms   30
both pale and glowing took possession of her young sense, and
fixed themselves associations which remained through her
after-years. Our moods are apt to bring with them images
which succeed each other like the magic-lantern pictures of a
doze; and in certain states of dull forlornness Dorothea all her   35
life continued to see the vastness of St Peter's, the huge bronze
canopy, the excited intention in the attitudes and garments of
the prophets and evangelists in the mosaics above, and the red
drapery which was being hung for Christmas spreading itself
everywhere like a disease of the retina.   40

GEORGE ELIOT, *Middlemarch*

1   How many facets of Rome does the writer attempt to establish
here? With what success?

2   In a passage which sets out to describe Dorothea's feelings
about Rome, some attention is given to the supposed feelings of
two other kinds of visitor. Consider the writer's motives.

3   How was Dorothea's attitude towards Rome affected by *a*) her
education, *b*) her character, *c*) her situation?

4   Are there any attempts to engage the reader's feelings in this passage?

5   Examine the images which describe Dorothea's states of mind. Trace the relationship between them. What mood do they induce?

6   Show how the statement 'whose quick emotions gave the most abstract things the quality of a pleasure or a pain' (lines 12–13) is developed in the imagery.

7   Comment on the following metaphors:

    broken revelations (line 6).

    this vast wreck of ambitious ideals (line 26)

8   By examining the diction, try to ascertain the writer's own feelings about Rome.

9   Analyse the structure of the second sentence (lines 5–16), paying special attention to the relationship between ideas, sound and rhythm.

B

E. M. Forster's heroine, Adela Quested, has gone out to India accompanied by Mrs Moore, the mother of a prospective fiancé, Ronny. Having suppressed her awareness of not being in love with Ronny, she has recently decided to marry him. In this episode, the two Englishwomen are on their way to Dr Aziz's picnic at the Marabar Caves, where the repressed instinctive side of Adela's nature is to rebel and bring about a breakdown which will have fateful consequences.

    'Anything to be seen of the hills?'

    'Only various shades of the dark.'

    'We can't be far from the place where my hyena was.' She peered into the timeless twilight. The train crossed a nullah. 'Pomper, pomper, pomper', was the sound that the wheels   5 made as they trundled over the bridge, moving very slowly. A hundred yards on came a second nullah, then a third, suggesting the neighbourhood of higher ground. 'Perhaps this is mine; anyhow, the road runs parallel with the railway.' Her accident was a pleasant memory; she felt in her dry, honest   10 way that it had given her a good shake up, and taught her Ronny's true worth. Then she went back to her plans; plans had been a passion with her from girlhood. Now and then she paid tribute to the present, said how friendly and intelligent Aziz was, ate a guava, couldn't eat a fried sweet, practised her   15 Urdu on the servant; but her thoughts ever veered to the manageable future, and to the Anglo-Indian life she had decided to endure. And as she appraised it with its adjuncts of Turtons and Burtons, the train accompanied her sentences, 'pomper, pomper', the train half asleep, going nowhere in   20 particular and with no passenger of importance in any of its carriages, the branch-line train, lost on a low embankment be- tween dull fields. Its message—for it had one—avoided her well- equipped mind. Far away behind her, with a shriek that meant business, rushed the Mail connecting up important towns such   25 as Calcutta and Lahore, where interesting events occur and personalities are developed. She understood that. Unfortunately, India has few important towns. India is the country, fields, fields then hills, jungle, hills and more fields. The branch line stops, the road is only practicable for cars to a point, the   30 bullock-carts lumber down the side tracks, paths fray out into the cultivation, and disappear near a splash of red paint. How can the mind take hold of such a country? Generations of invaders have tried, but they remain in exile. The important towns they build are only retreats, their quarrels the malaise   35 of men who cannot find their way home. India knows of their trouble. She knows of the whole world's trouble, to its uttermost depth. She calls 'Come' through her hundred mouths, through objects ridiculous and august. But come to what? She has never defined. She is not a promise, only an appeal.   40

    'I will fetch you from Simla when it's cool enough. I will unbottle you in fact', continued the reliable girl. 'We then see some of the Mogul stuff—how appalling if we let you miss the Taj!—and then I will see you off at Bombay. Your last glimpse

of this country really shall be interesting.' But Mrs Moore had   45
fallen asleep exhausted by the early start. . . . When she awoke,
Adela had ceased to plan and leant out of a window, saying,
'They're rather wonderful'.

Astonishing even from the rise of the civil station, here the
Marabar were gods to whom earth is a ghost. Kawa Dol was   50
nearest. It shot up in a single slab, on whose summit one rock
was poised—if a mass so great can be called one rock. Behind it,
recumbent, were the hills that contained the other caves,
isolated each from his neighbour by broad channels of the
plain. The assemblage, ten in all, shifted a little as the train   55
crept past them, as if observing its arrival.

'I'ld not have missed this for anything', said the girl,
exaggerating her enthusiasm. 'Look, the sun's rising—this'll
be absolutely magnificent—come quickly—look. I wouldn't
have missed this for anything. We should never have seen it   60
if we'd stuck to the Turtons and their eternal elephants.'

As she spoke, the sky to the left turned angry orange. Colour
throbbed and mounted behind a pattern of trees, grew in
intensity, was yet brighter, incredibly brighter, strained from
without against the globe of the air. They awaited the miracle.   65
But at the supreme moment, when night should have died and
day lived, nothing occurred. It was as if virtue had failed in the
celestial fount. The hues in the east decayed, the hills seemed
dimmer though in fact better lit, and a profound disappoint-
ment entered with the morning breeze. Why, when the chamber   70
was prepared, did the bridegroom not enter with trumpets and
shawms, as humanity expects? The sun rose without splendour.
He was presently observed trailing yellowish behind the trees,
or against insipid sky, and touching the bodies already at work
in the fields.   75

E. M. FORSTER, *A Passage to India*

1   Describe the personality of Adela, and consider the means by
which it is established in this passage.

2   Discuss the thematic significance of the gap between the
narrator's and Adela's views of her relationship to her surroundings.

3   Discuss the contributions made to the passage by a) what Mrs Moore says—'Only various shades of the dark' and b) what she does.

4   Consider the relationship between syntax and theme in the following sentences:

Now and then . . . decided to endure. (lines 13–18)
India is the country . . . and more fields. (lines 28–9)

5   What use does Forster make of the false dawn incident (lines 57–75)? Can the biblical allusion of the final paragraph be justified?

6   Consider the effect of the following:

trundled (line 6), a good shake up (line 11), lost (line 22), fray (line 31), appalling (line 43), crept (line 56), yellowish (line 73).

7   Are the elements of realism and symbol/fantasy compatible with each other?

COMPARATIVE STUDY

1   Compare the attitudes adopted by these writers towards a) their readers, and b) their heroines.

2   Examine the different ways in which they have attempted to establish meaningful contrasts within the situation they describe. Have they been successful?

3   Both George Eliot and E. M. Forster select elements from their material and present them as symbols of states of mind. How successful has each been in doing this?

4   Does E. M. Forster show greater psychological awareness than George Eliot, or is his freer use of symbolism only a reflection of the fact that he was writing fifty years later?

TEN

Moralists are not necessarily solemn, and when Evelyn Waugh died he was described as 'the funniest Englishman of his generation'. He also had a taste for administering shocks, and this is evident in the following passage from *A Handful of Dust*. A certain confusion over names is designed to give us a bizarre glimpse of Brenda's feelings. There are two Johns in her life: her lover, John Beaver, and her small son, John Andrew.

There was a little party at Lady Cockpurse's, Veronica, and Daisy and Sybil, Souki de Foucauld-Esterhazy, and four or five others, all women. They were there to consult a new fortune-teller called Mrs Northcote. Mrs Beaver had discovered her and for every five guineas that she earned at her introduction 5 Mrs Beaver took a commission of two pounds twelve and sixpence. She told fortunes in a new way, by reading the soles of the feet. They waited their turn impatiently. 'What a time she is taking over Daisy.'

'She is very thorough,' said Polly, 'and it tickles rather.' 10
Presently Daisy emerged. 'What was she like?' they asked.
'I mustn't tell or it spoils it all', said Daisy.

They had dealt cards for precedence. It was Brenda's turn now. She went next door to Mrs Northcote who was sitting at a stool beside an armchair. She was a dowdy, middle-aged 15 woman with a slightly genteel accent. Brenda sat down and took off her shoe and stocking. Mrs Northcote laid the foot on her knee and gazed at it with great solemnity; then she picked it up and began tracing the small creases of the sole with the point of a silver pencil case. Brenda wriggled her toes luxuriously 20 and settled down to listen.

Next door they said, 'Where's Mr Beaver today?'
'He's flown over to France with his mother to see some new

wallpapers. She's been worrying all day thinking he's had an
accident.'
'It's all very touching, isn't it? Though I can't see his point   25
myself . . .'
'You must never do anything on Thursdays', said Mrs
Northcote.
'Nothing?'
'Nothing important. You are intellectual, imaginative,   30
sympathetic, easily led by others, impulsive, affectionate. You
are highly artistic and not giving full scope to your capabilities.'
'Isn't there anything about love?'
'I am coming to love. All these lines from the great toe to the
instep represent lovers.'   35
'Yes, go on some more about that . . .'
Princess Abdul Akbar was announced. 'Where's Brenda?' she
said. 'I thought she'd be here.'
'Mrs Northcote's doing her now.'
'Jock Menzies wants to see her. He's downstairs.'   40
'Darling Jock . . . Why on earth didn't you bring him up?'
'No it's something terribly important. He's got to see
Brenda alone.'
'My dear, how mysterious. Well, she won't be long now.
We can't disturb them. It would upset Mrs Northcote.'   45
Jenny told them the news.
On the other side of the door, Brenda's leg was beginning to
feel slightly chilly. 'Four men dominate your fate', Mrs
Northcote was saying, 'one is loyal and tender but he has not
yet disclosed his love, one is passionate and overpowering,   50
you are a little afraid of him.'
'Dear me', said Brenda. 'How very exciting. Who can they be?'
'One you must avoid; he bodes no good for you, he is
steely hearted and rapacious.'
'I bet that's my Mr Beaver, bless him.'   55
Downstairs Jock was waiting in the small front room where
Polly's guests usually assembled before luncheon. It was five
past six.
Soon Brenda pulled on her stocking, stepped into her shoe
and joined the ladies. 'Most enjoyable', she pronounced.   60
'Why, how odd you all look.'

'Jock Grant-Menzies wants to see you downstairs.'

'Jock? How very extraordinary. It isn't anything awful, is it?'

'You'd better go and see him.'

Suddenly Brenda became frightened by the strange air of the   65
room and the unfamiliar expression in her friends' faces. She
ran downstairs to the room where Jock was waiting.

'What is it, Jock? Tell me quickly, I'm scared. It's nothing
awful, is it?'

'I'm afraid it is. There's been a very serious accident.'   70

'John?'

'Yes.'

'Dead?'

He nodded.   75

She sat down on a hard little Empire chair against the wall,
perfectly still with her hands folded in her lap, like a small
well-brought-up child introduced into a room full of grown-
ups. She said, 'Tell me what happened. Why do you know about
it first?'

'I've been down at Hetton since the week-end.'   80

'Hetton?'

'Don't you remember? John was going hunting today.'

She frowned, not at once taking in what he was saying.
'John . . . John Andrew . . . I . . . oh, thank God . . .' Then she
burst into tears.   85

She wept helplessly, turning round in the chair and
pressing her forehead against its gilt back.

Upstairs Mrs Northcote had Souki Foucauld-Esterhazy by
the foot and was saying, 'There are four men dominating your
fate. One is loyal and tender but has not yet disclosed his   90
love . . .'

EVELYN WAUGH, *A Handful of Dust*

1   What is the writer's attitude towards the events he is describing?

2   Comment on the following in their contexts:

     . . . for every five guineas that she earned at her introduction
Mrs Beaver took a commission of two pounds twelve and sixpence.
(lines 5–7)

Upstairs Mrs Northcote had Souki Foucauld-Esterhazy by the foot . . . (lines 88–9)

3   Consider the contrasts between the speeches of Mrs Northcote and those of the other women, and between the description of Mrs Northcote's background, manner and appearance and her activities. What are they intended to convey?

4   Analyse the function of the simile 'like a small well-brought-up child' (lines 77–8).

5   Discuss the use of descriptive detail.

6   Write a brief account of the narrative technique used in this passage.

ELEVEN

'I almost think that the gift of speech is too dangerous to use' says
Dudley Gaveston in Ivy Compton-Burnett's novel *A Family and a
Fortune*, and such sensitivity with regard to the spoken word suggests
that he is a character with whom the author has identified herself.
Miss Compton-Burnett has a higher reverence than most non-
dramatic writers for what her personages say: speech is virtually the
sole dimension of their existence. It is rarely the narrator who tells
us what they think and feel; and indications of appearance or
manner are reduced to the status of stage directions in a play. It has
always been the story-teller's right to *intervene* in the imaginary events
he is recounting: he will give detailed information about time and
place; lay bare motives and thoughts that are normally concealed;
and persuade the reader to adopt a particular attitude towards his
characters. By voluntarily foregoing the free exercise of these
privileges, Miss Compton-Burnett might seem to be inflicting
unnecessary privations on herself; but, in using a lens no wider
than is needed to record a series of dining-table conversations, she
focuses the reader's attention with unusual sharpness on the
situations which her dialogue gradually reveals.

Her novels are dark comedies of upper-class life at the turn of the
century. Her families are large and exceptionally articulate, and they
choose—or are forced—to turn in upon themselves. The gift of
speech may be 'dangerous' because it dwells on highly-charged
topics, but more often because it is the means by which a person
reveals (or betrays) his inner self, and the means by which he will
try to forge links (perhaps uncomfortably binding links) with the
people around him. During the course of *Daughters and Sons*, the
youngest member of the family, Muriel, progresses from giggles,
through questions which are criticized for being sham-conversation,
to the turning point at which she begins to make her own uninhibited—and dangerous—comments on the family situation

unfolding round her. By doing so she has become a fully-fledged
Compton-Burnett character.

One of the questions which presents itself when we analyse this
writer's technique is whether or not she is trying to create an
accurate 'imitation' of the surface of life. Drama has been mentioned;
but when we suggest that these novels resemble plays do we mean
that they have an Arthur Miller realism; or that they inhabit a genre
of elegant farce with *The Importance of Being Earnest*; or, as some critics
have suggested, that the insight, self-knowledge and articulateness of
her personages are literary conventions like the rhetoric one finds
in different forms in the plays of T. S. Eliot or J. M. Synge?

The following passage occurs shortly after the opening of A Family and a Fortune
(published in 1939*). The Gaveston family are at breakfast. Edgar and Blanche
have four children. The eldest, Justine, is thirty; Edgar is twenty-eight, Clement
twenty-six and Aubrey fifteen. Dudley is Edgar's younger brother.*

'How did you sleep, Father?' said Justine.

'Very well, my dear; I think I can say well. I slept for some
hours. I hope you have a good account to give.'

'Oh, don't ask about the sleep of a healthy young woman,
Father. Trust you to worry about the sleep of your only   5
daughter!' Edgar flinched in proportion to his doubt how far
this confidence was justified. 'It is your sleep that matters, and I
am not half satisfied about it.'

'The young need sleep, my dear.'

'Oh, I am not as young as all that. A ripe thirty, and all my   10
years lived to the full! I would not have missed one of them.
I don't rank myself with the callow young any longer.'

'Always Father's little girl', murmured Aubrey.

'What my son?' said Edgar.

'I still rank myself with the young', said Aubrey, as if   15
repeating what he had said. 'I think I had better until I go to
school. Anything else would make me look silly, and Clement
would not like me to look that.'

'Get on with your breakfast, little boy,' said Justine. 'Straight
on and not another word until you have finished.'   20

'I was making my little effort to keep the ball of conversation
rolling. Every little counts.'

'So it does, dear, and with all our hearts we acknowledge it.'
Blanche smiled from her eldest to her youngest child in
appreciation of their feeling.   25
'Aubrey meets with continual success', said Mark. 'He is
indeed a kind of success in himself.'
'What kind?' said Clement.
'Too simple, Clement,' said Justine, shaking her head. 'How
did you sleep, Uncle?'   30
'Very well until I was awakened by the rain. Then I went to
the window and stood looking out into the night. I see now
that people really do that.'
'They really shut out the air', said Clement.
'Is Clement a soured young man?' said Aubrey.   35
'I had a very bad night', said Blanche, in a mild, conversa-
tional tone, without complaint that no enquiry had been made
of her. 'I have almost forgotten what it is to have a good one.'
'Poor little Mother! But you sleep in the afternoon', said
Justine.   40
'I never do. I have my rest, of course; I could not get on
without it. But I never sleep. I may close my eyes to ease them,
but I am always awake.'
'You were snoring yesterday, Mother,' said Justine, with the
insistence upon people's sleeping and giving this sign, which   45
seems to be a human characteristic.
'No, I was not', said Blanche, with the annoyance at the
course, which is unfortunately another. 'I never snore even at
night, so I certainly do not when I am just resting in the day.'
'Mother, I tiptoed in and you did not give a sign.'   50
'If you made no sound, and I was resting my eyes, I may not
have heard you, of course.'
'Anyhow a few minutes in the day do not make up for a bad
night', said Mark.
'But I do not sleep in the day, even for a few minutes', said   55
his mother in a shriller tone. 'I don't know what to say to make
you all understand.'
'I don't know why people mind admitting to a few minutes'
sleep in the day,' said Dudley, 'when we all acknowledge hours
at night and indeed require compassion if we do not have   60
them.'

'Who has acknowledged them?' said Clement. 'It will appear that as a family we do without sleep.'

'But I do not mind admitting to them', said Blanche. 'What I mean is that it is not the truth. There is no point in not speaking the truth even about a trivial matter.'

'I do not describe insomnia in that way', said Mark.

'Dear boy, you do understand', said Blanche, holding out her hand with an almost wild air. 'You do prevent me feeling quite alone.'

'Come, come, Mother, I was tactless, I admit,' said Justine. 'I know people hate confessing that they sleep in the day. I ought to have remembered it.'

'Justine now shows tact', murmured Aubrey.

'It is possible—it seems to be possible', said Edgar, 'to be resting with closed eyes and give the impression of sleep.'

'You forget the snoring, Father,' said Justine, in a voice so low and light as to escape her mother's ears.

'If you don't forget it too, I don't know what we are to do', said Mark, in the same manner.

'Snoring is not a proof of being asleep', said Dudley.

'But I was not snoring', said Blanche, in the easier tone of one losing grasp of a situation. 'I should have known it myself. It would not be possible to be awake and make a noise and not hear it.'

Justine gave an arch look at anyone who would receive it. Edgar did so as a duty and rapidly withdrew his eyes as another.

'Why do we not learn that no one ever snores under any circumstances?' said Clement.

'I wonder how the idea of snoring arose', said Mark.

'Mother, are you going to eat no more than that?' said Justine. 'You are not ashamed of eating as well as of sleeping, I hope.'

'There has been no question of sleeping. And I am not ashamed of either. I always eat very well and I always sleep very badly. There is no connection between them.'

'You seem to be making an exception in the first matter today', said her husband.

'Well, it upsets me to be contradicted, Edgar, and told that I do things when I don't do them, and when I know quite

well what I do, myself', said Blanche, almost flouncing in her
chair.

'It certainly does, Mother dear. So we will leave it at that;
that you know quite well what you do yourself.'

'It seems a reasonable conclusion', said Mark.

'I believe people always know that best', said Dudley. 'If we   105
could see ourselves as others see us, we should be much more
misled, though people always talk as if we ought to try to do
it.'

'They want us to be misled and cruelly', said his nephew.

'I don't know', said Justine. 'We might often meet a good,
sound, impartial judgment.'   110

'And we know, when we have one described like that, what a
dreadful judgment it is', said her uncle.

'Half the truth, the blackest of lies', said Mark.

'The whitest of lies really', said Clement. 'Or there is no such
thing as a white lie.'   115

'Well, there is not', said his sister. 'Truth is truth and a lie is
a lie.'

'What is Truth?' said Aubrey. 'Has Justine told us?'

'Truth is whatever happens to be true under the circumstances', said his sister, doing so at the moment. 'We ought not   120
to mind a searchlight being turned on our inner selves, if we
are honest about them.'

'That is our reason', said Mark. ' "Know thyself" is a most
superfluous direction. We can't avoid it.'

'We can only hope that no one else knows', said Dudley.   125

'Uncle, what nonsense!' said Justine. 'You are the most
transparent and genuine person, the very last to say that.'

'What do you all really mean?' said Edgar, speaking rather
hurriedly, as if to check any further personal description.

'I think I only mean', said his brother, 'that human beings   130
ought always to be judged very tenderly, and that no one will
be as tender as themselves. "Remember what you owe to
yourself" is another piece of superfluous advice.'

'But better than most advice', said Aubrey, lowering his
voice as he ended. 'More tender.'   135

'Now, little boy, hurry up with your breakfast', said Justine.
'Mr Penrose will be here in a few minutes.'

'To pursue his life work of improving Aubrey', said Clement.

'Clement ought to have ended with a sigh', said Aubrey. 140 'But I daresay the work has its own unexpected rewards.'

'I forget what I learned at Eton', said his uncle.

'Yes, so do I; yes, so to a great extent do I', said Edgar. 'Yes, I believe I forgot the greater part of it.'

'You can't really have lost it, Father,' said Justine. 'An 145 education in the greatest school in the world must have left its trace. It must have contributed to your forming.'

'It does not seem to matter that I can't go to school', said Aubrey. 'It will be a shorter cut to the same end.'

'Now, little boy, don't take that obvious line. And remember 150 that self-education is the greatest school of all.

'And education by Penrose? What is that?'

'Say Mr Penrose. And get on with your breakfast.'

'He has only had one piece of toast', said Blanche in a tone which suggested that it would be one of despair if the situation 155 were not familiar. 'And he is a growing boy.'

'I should not describe him in those terms', said Mark.

'I should be at a loss to describe him', said Clement.

'Don't be silly', said their mother at once. 'You are both of you just as difficult to describe.'   160

'Some people defy description', said Aubrey. 'Uncle and I are among them.'

'There is something in it', said Justine, looking round.

'Perhaps we should not—it may be as well not to discuss people who are present', said Edgar.   165

'Right as usual, Father. I wish the boys would emulate you.'

'Oh, I think they do, dear', said Blanche, in an automatic tone. 'I see a great likeness in them both to their father. It gets more striking.'

'And does no one think poor Uncle a worthy object of 170 emulation? He is as experienced and polished a person as Father.'

Edgar looked up at this swift disregard of accepted advice.

'I am a changeling', said Dudley. 'Aubrey and I are very hard to get hold of.'

175

'And you can't send a person you can't put your finger on to school', said his nephew.

'You can see that he does the next best thing', said Justine. 'Off with you at once. There is Mr Penrose on the steps. Don't keep the poor little man waiting.'   180

'Justine refers to every other person as poor', said Clement.

'Well, I am not quite without the bowels of human compassion. The ups and downs of the world do strike me, I confess.'

'Chiefly the downs.'   185

'Well, there are more of them.'

'Poor little man', murmured Aubrey, leaving his seat. 'Whose little man is he? I am Justine's little boy.'

'It seems—is it not rather soon after breakfast to work?' said Edgar.   190

'They go for a walk first, as you know, Father. It is good for Aubrey to have a little adult conversation apart from his family. I asked Mr Penrose to make the talk educational.'

'Did you, dear?' said Blanche, contracting her eyes. 'I think you should leave that kind of thing to Father or me.'   195

'Indeed I should not, Mother. And not have it done at all? That would be a nice alternative. I should do all I can for you all, as it comes into my head, as I always have and always shall. Don't try to prevent what is useful and right.'

Blanche subsided under this reasonable direction.   200

'Now off with you both! Off to your occupations', said Justine, waving her hand towards her brothers. 'I hope you have some. I have, and they will not wait.'

'I am glad I have none', said Dudley. 'I could not bear to have regular employment.'   205

IVY COMPTON-BURNETT, *A Family and a Fortune*

1   Describe the character of Justine. To what extent does your awareness of her as a person depend upon:

    a) what she says
    b) how she says it
    c) what other members of the family say about or to her and
    d) what the author suggests we should feel about her?

2   Explore the relationships between Justine and each other
member of the family. How have they been conveyed?

3   Apart from Justine, are any other speakers identified by their
manner (as opposed to matter)?

4   To which speaker would you ascribe the unattributed remark
in line 23? Why?

5   Consider the role of the following remarks in helping to
establish the personality of the speakers:

   a) Mark: 'Anyhow a few minutes in the day do not make up for
   a bad night' (lines 53–4)
   b) Blanche: 'I don't know what to say to make you all understand' (lines 56–7)
   c) Aubrey: 'Justine now shows tact' (line 74)
   d) Dudley: 'I think I only mean . . . that human beings ought
   always to be judged very tenderly . . .' (lines 130–1)
   e) Clement: 'To pursue his life work of improving Aubrey'
   (line 138)
   f) Edgar: 'Yes, so do I; yes, so to a great extent do I . . . Yes,
   I believe I forgot the greater part of it' (lines 143–4)
   g) Justine: 'Don't try to prevent what is useful and right'
   (line 199)

6   Do you think we are expected to agree with Aubrey when he
describes Clement as a 'soured young man'?

7   Examine the function of the commentaries attached to
Blanche's remarks in lines 36–8, 46–7, 55–6, 68–9, 82–3 and
101–2.

8   Ivy Compton-Burnett's characters continually challenge the
assumptions of various philosophies of life. Dudley suggests that
he has done so when he says 'I see now that people really do that'
(lines 32–3). What is he referring to? Can you find other examples
of this sort of questioning in the passage?

9   'Justine gave an arch look at anyone who would receive it.
Edgar did so as a duty and rapidly withdrew his eyes as another'
(lines 86–7). Could you defend these two sentences if it were
claimed that they were cryptic and obscure?

10   To what kind of drama does this passage have the closest

affinity? If you were dramatizing *A Family and a Fortune* and had the choice of either television or sound radio as your medium, which would you prefer?

11   What are the advantages of this method of telling a story?

12   'Ivy Compton-Burnett's skill is most clearly demonstrated in the tension she maintains between the apparently natural flow of her table-talk and its turning-points, crescendoes and climaxes.' Is this comment borne out by the extract?

TWELVE

A

He gasped a minute, and that gave her time to say: 'You
see, Mr Owen, how impossible it is to talk of such things
yet!'

Like lightning he had grasped her arm. 'You mean you will
talk of them?' Then as he began to take the flood of assent from
her eyes: 'You will listen to me? Oh, you dear, you dear—   5
when, when?'

'Ah, when it isn't mere misery!' The words had broken from
her in a sudden loud cry, and what next happened was that the
very sound of her pain upset her. She heard her own true note;
she turned short away from him; in a moment she had burst   10
into sobs; in another his arms were round her; the next she
had let herself go so far that even Mrs Gereth might have seen
it. He clasped her, and she gave herself—she poured out her
tears on his breast; something prisoned and pent throbbed
and gushed; something deep and sweet surged up—something   15
that came from far within and far off, that had begun with the
sight of him in his indifference and had never had rest since
then. The surrender was short, but the relief was long; she felt
his lips upon her face and his arms tightened with his full
divination. What she did, what she had done, she scarcely knew: 20
she only was aware, as she broke from him again, of what had
taken place in his own quick breast. What had taken place was
that, with the click of a spring, he saw. He had cleared the high
wall at a bound; it was as if a whirlwind had come and gone,
laying low the great false front that she had built up stone by   25
stone. The strangest thing of all was the momentary sense of
desolation.

'Ah, all the while you cared?' Owen read the truth with a
wonder so great that it was visibly almost a sadness, a terror

caused by his sudden perception of where the impossibility was   30
not. That made it all perhaps elsewhere.

'I cared, I cared, I cared!' Fleda moaned it as defiantly as if
she were confessing a misdeed. 'How couldn't I care? But you
mustn't, you must never, never ask! It isn't for us to talk
about!' she insisted. 'Don't speak of it, don't speak!'   35

It was easy indeed not to speak when the difficulty was to
find words. He clasped his hands before her as he might have
clasped them at an altar; his pressed palms shook together while
he held his breath and while she stilled herself in the effort to
come round again to the real and the right. He helped this   40
effort, soothing her into a seat with a touch as light as if she had
really been something sacred. She sank into a chair and he
dropped before her on his knees; she fell back with closed eyes
and he buried his face in her lap. There was no way to thank
her but this act of prostration, which lasted, in silence, till she   45
laid consenting hands on him, touched his head and stroked it,
held it in her tenderness till he acknowledged his long
density. He made the avowal seem only his—made her, when
she rose again, raise him at last, softly, as if from the abasement
of shame. If in each other's eyes now, however, they saw the   50
truth, this truth, to Fleda, looked harder even than before—
all the harder that when, at the very moment she recognized it,
he murmured to her ecstatically, in fresh possession of her
hands, which he drew up to his breast, holding them tight
there with both his own: 'I'm saved, I'm saved—I am.'   55

HENRY JAMES, *The Spoils of Poynton*

1   Has the writer succeeded in his portrayal, of emotional stress
in paragraph 3 (lines 7–27)?

2   Examine
   a) the dialogue
   b) the diction of the sentence 'She sank into a chair and he
   dropped before her on his knees; she fell back with closed eyes
   and he buried his face in her lap.'
   c) the syntax of the final sentence

3   Trace the development of the liturgical imagery in the final

paragraph. What is it intended to convey? Do you consider it well chosen for its purpose?

4   Comment on the effectiveness of
    a) She heard her own true note (line 9)
    b) That made it all perhaps elsewhere (line 31)

5   Can the following be justified?
    The use of the past perfect tense, 'soothing her into a seat' (line 41), 'softly' (line 49), 'in fresh possession of her hands' (lines 53–4).

B

Miss Vincy was alone, and blushed so deeply when Lydgate came in that he felt a corresponding embarrassment, and instead of any playfulness, he began at once to speak of his reason for calling, and to beg her, almost formally, to deliver the message to her father. Rosamond, who at the first moment   5 felt as if her happiness were returning, was keenly hurt by Lydgate's manner; her blush had departed, and she assented coldly, without adding an unnecessary word, some trivial chain-work which she had in her hands enabling her to avoid looking at Lydgate higher than his chin. In all failures, the   10 beginning is certainly the half of the whole. After sitting two long moments while he moved his whip and could say nothing, Lydgate rose to go, and Rosamond, made nervous by her struggle between mortification and the wish not to betray it, dropped her chain as if startled, and rose too, mechanically.   15 Lydgate instantaneously stooped to pick up the chain. When he rose he was very near to a lovely little face set on a fair long neck which he had been used to see turning about under the most perfect management of self-contented grace. But as he raised his eyes now he saw a certain helpless quivering which   20 touched him quite newly, and made him look at Rosamond with a questioning flash. At this moment she was as natural as

she had ever been when she was five years old; she felt that her
tears had risen, and it was no use to try to do anything else
than let them stay like water on a blue flower or let them fall   25
over her cheeks, even as they would.

That moment of naturalness was the crystallizing feather-
touch: it shook flirtation into love. Remember that the
ambitious man who was looking at those Forget-me-nots under
the water was very warm-hearted and rash. He did not know   30
where the chain went; an idea had thrilled through the
recesses within him which had a miraculous effect in raising
the power of passionate love lying buried there in no sealed
sepulchre, but under the lightest, easily pierced mould. His
words were quite abrupt and awkward; but the tone made   35
them sound like an ardent, appealing avowal.

'What is the matter? you are distressed. Tell me—pray.'

Rosamond had never been spoken to in such tones before.
I am not sure that she knew what the words were; but she
looked at Lydgate and the tears fell over her cheeks. There   40
could have been no more complete answer than that silence,
and Lydgate, forgetting everything else, completely mastered
by the outrush of tenderness at the sudden belief that this sweet
young creature depended on him for her joy, actually put his
arms round her, folding her gently and protectingly—he was   45
used to being gentle with the weak and suffering—and kissed
each of the two large tears. This was a strange way of arriving
at an understanding, but it was a short way. Rosamond was not
angry, but she moved backward a little in timid happiness, and
Lydgate could now sit near her and speak less incompletely.   50
Rosamond had to make her little confession, and he poured out
words of gratitude and tenderness with impulsive lavishment.
In half an hour he left the house an engaged man, whose soul
was not his own, but the woman's to whom he had bound
himself.   55

GEORGE ELIOT, *Middlemarch*

1   'A love scene with the narrator as intruder.' Can the intrusion
be justified?

2   Dr Lydgate's marriage to Rosamond will be unhappy. Analyse

the means by which the writer conveys her attitude to the coming engagement in paragraph 2.

3   What impression do we receive of
     a) Rosamond's appearance and b) her character?
     How have these impressions been conveyed?

4   Comment on the effectiveness of the following:
     Lydgate instantaneously stooped to pick up the chain (line 16)
     he was used to being gentle with the weak and suffering (lines 45–6)
     In half an hour he left the house an engaged man, whose soul was not his own, but the woman's to whom he had bound himself (lines 53–5)

5   Consider the following words and phrases in their contexts. Do you think they were well chosen?
     certain (line 20), even as they would (line 26), actually (line 44), little (line 51)

COMPARATIVE STUDY

1   'Success or failure here is initially a matter of narrative perspective, i.e. where the narrator stands in relation to the characters and events he describes.' Discuss.

2   Make a comparative study of the use of imagery in these passages.

3   Which do you prefer?

THIRTEEN

In B from *Sanctuary* (1931), Faulkner uses a descriptive technique
which he might have learned from Herman Melville, the author of
A, *Moby Dick* (1851). Both descriptions are poetic rather than
naturalistic. The accumulation of detail in each is deceptive, and
the final result is truth of atmosphere rather than the photographic
sharpness we might have expected. In each case the mood generated
is in harmony with the events described in their respective episodes.

A

Crossing this dusky entry, and on through yon low-arched
way—cut through what in old times must have been a great
central chimney with fire-places all round—you enter the
public room. A still duskier place is this, with such low
ponderous beams above, and such old wrinkled planks   5
beneath, that you could almost fancy you trod some old craft's
cock-pits, especially of such a howling night, when this
corner-anchored old ark rocked so furiously. On one side
stood a long, low shelf-like table covered with cracked glass
cases, filled with dusty rarities gathered from this wide world's   10
remotest nooks. Projecting from the further angle of the room
stands a dark-looking den—the bar—a rude attempt at a right
whale's head. Be that how it may, there stands the vast arched
bone of the whale's jaw, so wide, a coach might drive beneath
it. Within are shabby shelves, ranged round with old decanters,   15
bottles, flasks; and in those jaws of swift destruction, like
another cursed Jonah (by which name indeed they called him),

bustles a little withered old man, who, for their money, dearly
sells the sailors deliriums and death.

Abominable are the tumblers into which he pours his   20
poison. Though true cylinders without—within, the villainous
green goggling glasses deceitfully tapered downwards to a
cheating bottom. Parallel meridians rudely pecked into the
glass, surround these footpad's goblets. Fill to this mark, and
your charge is but a penny; to this a penny more; and so on to   25
the full glass—the Cape Horn measure, which you may gulp
down for a shilling.

Upon entering the place I found a number of young
seamen gathered about a table, examining by a dim light divers
specimens of skrimshander. I sought the landlord, and telling   30
him I desired to be accommodated with a room, received for
answer that his house was full—not a bed unoccupied. 'But
avast,' he added, tapping his forehead, 'you haint no objections
to sharing a harpooneer's blanket, have ye? I s'pose you are
goin' a whalin', so you'd better get used to that sort of thing.'   35

HERMAN MELVILLE, Moby Dick

1   Describe the various means by which Melville suggests, in this
extract from his third chapter, that Moby Dick will be concerned with
the sea and whaling.

2   Comment on the use of adjectives in the first paragraph.

3   What kind of relationship with the reader is Melville trying to
establish, and what means does he use to this end?

4   Consider his use of fantasy, allusion and metaphor.

5   On what grounds would you either defend or attack the style of
this passage?

B

They reached Memphis in mid-afternoon. At the foot of the
bluff below Main Street Popeye turned into a narrow street of

smoke-grimed frame houses with tiers of wooden galleries, set
a little back in grassless plots, with now and then a forlorn and
hardy tree of some shabby species—gaunt, lopbranched   5
magnolias, a stunted elm, or a locust in greyish, cadaverous
bloom—interspersed by rear ends of garages; a scrap-heap in
a vacant lot; a low-doored cavern of an equivocal appearance
where an oilcloth-covered counter and a row of backless stools,
a metal coffee-urn, and a fat man in a dirty apron with a   10
toothpick in his mouth, stood for an instant out of the gloom
with an effect as of a sinister and meaningless photograph
poorly made. From the bluff, beyond a line of office buildings
terraced sharply against the sunfilled sky, came a sound of
traffic—motor horns, trolleys—passing overhead on the river   15
breeze; at the end of the street a trolley materialized in the
narrow gap with an effect as of magic and vanished with a
stupendous clatter. On a second-storey gallery a young
Negress in her underclothes smoked a cigarette sullenly, her
arms on the balustrade.   20

Popeye drew up before one of the dingy three-storey houses,
the entrance of which was hidden by a dingy lattice cubicle
leaning a little awry. In the grimy grassplot before it two of
those small, woolly, white, worm-like dogs, one with a pink,
the other a blue, ribbon about its neck, moved about with an   25
air of sluggish and obscene paradox. In the sunlight their coats
looked as though they had been cleaned with gasoline.

Later Temple could hear them outside her door, whimpering
and scuffing, or, rushing thickly in when the Negro maid
opened the door, climbing and sprawling on to the bed and into 30
Miss Reba's lap with wheezy, flatulent sounds, billowing into
the rich pneumasis of her breast and tonguing along the metal
tankard which she waved in one ringed hand as she talked.

WILLIAM FAULKNER, *Sanctuary*

1   Consider the importance of contrast in this passage.

2   Examine Faulkner's use of metaphor and other kinds of
comparison.

3   Consider the effect of the following in their contexts:

cadaverous (line 6), equivocal (line 8), materialized (line 16), obscene (line 26)

4   Does Faulkner succeed in giving relevance to the details of his description?

5   Analyse the diction of paragraph 3, and consider its contribution to the mood of the passage.

COMPARATIVE STUDY

1   Make a comparative study of these passages, paying special attention to the means by which mood and atmosphere have been created.

2   'Two writers who are related to each other by their descriptive technique as well as their (American) nationality.' Do you agree?

3   What elements in these passages give them their poetic quality?

4   Consider the way in which both writers convey their feelings about the places they describe. Does this add to or detract from the effectiveness of the descriptions?

5   What kind of anticipation of future events does each passage inspire?

FOURTEEN

Samuel Richardson has been described as the 'father of the English novel'. The publication of *Pamela* in 1740 was certainly a turning point, and Richardson's attempt to identify himself with his heroine might be regarded as a feat of impersonation. The novel is organized as a series of letters written by a servant-girl to her parents. Both Mary Webb's *Precious Bane* (1924) and Joyce Cary's *Herself Surprised* (1941) have something of *Pamela* in their ancestry.

A

Having attracted the attention of an unscrupulous employer, the virtuous Pamela has been carried off to a country house where she finds herself in the 'care' of the unpleasant Mrs Jewkes.

She said she would go down to order supper, and insisted upon my company. I would have excused myself; but she put on a commanding air, that I durst not oppose. When I went down, she took me by the hand, and presented me to the most hideous monster I ever saw in my life. 'Here, Monsieur   5
Colbrand,' said she, 'here is your pretty ward and mine; let us try to make her time with us easy.' He bowed, put in his foreign grimaces, and, in broken English, told me, 'I was happy in de affections of de vinest gentleman in de varld!' I was quite frightened, and ready to drop down; I will describe him to you,   10
my dear father and mother, and you shall judge if I had not reason to be alarmed, as I was apprised of his hated employment, to watch me closer.
 He is a giant of a man for stature; taller by a good deal than Harry Mawlidge, in your neighbourhood, and large-boned,   15
scraggy, and has a hand!—I never saw such an one in my life.

He has great staring eyes, like the bull's that frightened me so;
vast jaw-bones sticking out; eyebrows hanging over his eyes;
two great scars upon his forehead, and one on his left cheek;
two large whiskers, and a monstrous wide mouth; blubber   20
lips, long yellow teeth, and a hideous grin. He wears his own
frightful long hair, tied up in a great black bag; a black crape
neckcloth, about a long ugly neck; and his throat sticking out
like a wen. As to the rest, he was dressed well enough, and had
a sword on, with a nasty red knot to it; leather gaiters,   25
buckled below his knees; and a foot near as long as my arm, I
verily think.

He said, he fright de lady, and offered to withdraw; but she
bid him not. I told Mrs Jewkes, that, as she knew I had been
crying, she should not have called me to the gentleman,   30
without letting me know he was there. I soon went up to my
closet, for my heart ached all the time I was at table, not
being able to look upon him without horror; and this brute of
a woman, though she saw my distress, before this addition to it,
no doubt did it on purpose to strike more terror into me. And   35
indeed it had its effect; for when I went to bed, I could think of
nothing but this hideous person, and my master's more
hideous actions; and thought them well paired.

SAMUEL RICHARDSON, Pamela

What is this writer attempting to do? What problems does he
create for himself in choosing this narrative form? How successful
has he been in overcoming them?

B

The heroine of Precious Bane, a farmer's daughter, describes a second encounter
with the man she has fallen in love with. Her interest in faces may spring partly
from the fact that she has never been allowed to forget her own facial deformity.

The men all turned towards Kester when he came up, and
Farmer Huglet, the chief of them called out:

'Where's your dawg?'

Mister Huglet was a great raw-looking man who seemed as if he'd come together accidental and was made up of two or three other people's bodies. He was a giant, very nearly, and clumsy, with tremendous long arms, and so big round the middle that tailors who brought their own stuff always charged extra for his clothes. He's got a mouth like a frog, and a round red snub nose, and such little eyes that they were lost in the mountains of flesh that made up his face. Whenever he couldna understand anything, he laughed, and his laugh was enough to frighten you. It came pretty often too. Grimble was hand-in-glove with him, and while Huglet stuck his red nose in the air, Grimble kept his long pale one down, so between them they didna miss much. They'd each got two dogs.

'Why, it's weaver', says Grimble. 'Dunna you know weaver, Huglet?'

'Why, no, we hanna crossed paths afore. My brother-in-law weaves for me, you mind. Well, weaver, where's your dawg?'

'I've got none.'

'No dawg? Stand aside, then.'

But he stood where he was. It so happened that he was about at the mid of the half-moon of grey stone that made the bull-ring, and the men with the dogs fell away a bit on either hand, so he was alone. Standing there so slim and straight in his green coat, with the airs blowing his hair a bit, so that a lock of it fell o'er his brow, his hat being under arm, he seemed to have naught to do with any there, but to be a part of the fair meadow, that matched his coat. He wore no beard nor whiskers, so you could see the shape and colour and the lines of all his face, which seemed to me to be a face you could never tire of looking on. Times I wonder if heaven will be thus, a long gazing on a face you canna tire of, but must ever have one more glimpse.

MARY WEBB, *Precious Bane*

Does the personality of the narrator detract from or add to the effectiveness of this passage?

C

Sarah Munday, the cook-heroine of Herself Suprised, has recently married her
employer's son, Matt. Here she meets Mr Hickson who, like herself, is a key figure
in Joyce Cary's Horse's Mouth trilogy.

Yet he was not so bad-looking a man; neither crooked nor
bald. He was on the short side and his head was on the big
side, with a very big face, and big nose. But he had very good
eyes, brown and clear, and a handsome chin with a cleft. His
teeth, too, were beautiful; too good for a man and nearly as   5
good as my own. As for his complexion, true, it was rough
and brown, like coffee, and full of holes from smallpox
because he had been born and brought up in Africa, but that
did him no harm in my eyes. I never liked pretty boys. A man's
face should be for use in battering at the world, and show the   10
scars of it.

   Now whether it was because I was a bride, or so much
talked about as the cook who married upwards, Mr Hickson
stayed chatting for ten minutes and showed by many signs
that he was ready to know me better. He said, too that he had   15
known my husband for many years; and was delighted to
know me.

   All this, I admit, was a triumph to a silly young girl, for Mr
Hickson was the greatest man in Bradnall; and as Matt said,
he used to go among us, especially at bazaars, with a face of   20
duty. He was affable as any prince, but you saw that you were
of his daily work and not of his pleasure. And there he was
talking to me with his hands in his pockets and his eyes
jumping about, and standing on his heels and laughing with
all his teeth, like any boy that has just picked up a belle at   25
I Spy corner. All the other ladies, and especially poor Maul,
were smiling one way at their customers, and looking the
other, with their eyes, at poor me and my conquest. And
so it was. For to my great surprise, while I was still planning
how to bring great Jack to the jug, as they say, and trying to   30
get Matt up to a garden-party, which would not fix Mr Hickson
to an hour and which would bring in all the doubting ones to

see him, he walked in to tea, all by himself, as cool as you
please. Imagine Matt's surprise when he came home at half-
past six and found me talking art with Mr Hickson, and Mr   35
Hickson hanging upon my words as if I had been his doting-
piece these four days.

Now I know nothing of art, as I told Mr Hickson, who was
a great collector and had his houses full of pictures; but he
made me talk, all the same, of what I liked, such as Marcus   40
Stone and Raphael; and also of my young life in the country
and that sweet land where I was reared.

Matt, as I say, was amazed. Yet I was glad to see how, shy as
he was, he came out when Mr Hickson used his fascinations
upon him, and talked and laughed. I had been afraid of Matt's   45
fumbling and stumbling with him. But no, and this was the
advantage of his good education, for though he was shy, he
knew himself Mr Hickson's equal, and could say, 'when I was
at the varsity', to which Mr Hickson would answer that he had
been there too.   50

JOYCE CARY, *Herself Surprised*

1   'The cook who married upwards'—has the writer remembered
his narrator's background in the ideas and style of this passage?

2   Does the writer give us any opportunities to dissociate
ourselves from the narrator and see this situation from an independent viewpoint?

COMPARATIVE STUDY

1   Examine the relationship of the modern passages, B and C, to
passage A.

2   Make a comparative study of B and C. Which is the more
successful?

FIFTEEN

The following passages have been taken from the fourth part of James Joyce's autobiographical novel, *A Portrait of the Artist as a Young Man.* Stephen Dedalus, the hero, is at a turning point in his life. He is about to leave school. He has recently undergone a conversion, has tried to live like an ascetic, and contemplated entering the Church. But he has decided not to enter the seminary, and as he walks in the direction of the sea, trying to suppress the agitation with which he is awaiting the result of an application to go to the university, he asks 'Why?'

Joyce chooses not to answer this question directly. Instead, he describes what the young man sees as he walks, and attempts to strike a balance between the inner world which is opening out to Stephen through introspection and the outer world which has begun to play upon his senses.

A

He turned seaward from the road at Dollymount and as he passed on to the thin wooden bridge he felt the planks shaking with the tramp of heavily shod feet. A squad of christian brothers was on its way back from the Bull and had begun to pass, two by two, across the bridge. Soon the whole bridge was   5 trembling and resounding. The uncouth faces passed him two by two, stained yellow or red or livid by the sea, and, as he strove to look at them with ease and indifference, a faint stain of personal shame and commiseration rose to his own face. Angry with himself he tried to hide his face from their eyes by   10

gazing sideways into the shallow swirling water under the
bridge but he still saw a reflection therein of their top-heavy
silk hats and humble tape-like collars and loosely-hanging
clerical clothes.

> —Brother Hickey   15
> Brother Quaid
> Brother MacArdle
> Brother Keogh—

Their piety would be like their names, like their faces, like
their clothes, and it was idle for him to tell himself that their   20
humble and contrite hearts, it might be, paid a far richer
tribute of devotion than his had ever been, a gift tenfold more
acceptable than his elaborate adoration. It was idle for him to
move himself to be generous towards them, to tell himself
that if he ever came to their gates, stripped of his pride, beaten   25
and in beggar's weeds, that they would be generous towards
him, loving him as themselves. Idle and embittering, finally,
to argue, against his own dispassionate certitude, that the
commandment of love bade us not to love our neighbour as
ourselves with the same amount and intensity of love but to   30
love him as ourselves with the same kind of love.

He drew forth a phrase from his treasure and spoke it softly
to himself:

> —A day of dappled seaborne clouds.

The phrase and the day and the scene harmonized in a chord.   35
Words. Was it their colours? He allowed them to glow and
fade, hue after hue: sunrise gold, the russet and green of apple
orchards, azure of waves, the grey-fringed fleece of clouds. No,
it was not their colours: it was the poise and balance of the
period itself. Did he then love the rhythmic rise and fall of   40
words better than their associations of legend and colour? Or
was it that, being as weak of sight as he was shy of mind, he
drew less pleasure from the reflection of the glowing sensible
world through the prism of a language many-coloured and
richly storied than from the contemplation of an inner world   45
of individual emotions mirrored perfectly in a lucid supple
periodic prose?

He passed from the trembling bridge on to firm land again.

At that instant, as it seemed to him, the air was chilled and,
looking askance towards the water, he saw a flying squall   50
darkening and crisping suddenly the tide. A faint click at his
heart, a faint throb in his throat told him once more of how his
flesh dreaded the cold infrahuman odour of the sea; yet he did
not strike across the downs on his left but held straight on along
the spine of rocks that pointed against the river's mouth.   55

JAMES JOYCE, *A Portrait of the Artist as a Young Man*

1   Are there any hints of Stephen's revulsion against the idea of
life as a religious in the diction of the first paragraph?

2   'Their piety would be like their names, like their faces, like
their clothes . . .' Has Joyce prepared the ground sufficiently for this
statement?

3   Are the hints of biblical and liturgical language in paragraph
2 conscious or unconscious? If they are there by design, what
function are they fulfilling?

4   What light does the word 'treasure' shed on Stephen's personality (line 32)?

5   Consider the sequence of colours in lines 37–8. In what
manner have they been applied to the line of verse?

6   Consider the implication of the chord and prism metaphors in the
penultimate paragraph. Has their use enabled Joyce to widen our
knowledge of Stephen's experience? Has the prism metaphor been
suggested elsewhere in the paragraph? Does it tell us anything about
the nature of language?

7   Analyse the parts played by sound and rhythm (including
word order) in the sentence, 'At that instant . . .' (lines 49–51).

B

He was alone. He was unheeded, happy and near to the wild
heart of life. He was alone and young and wilful and wild-

hearted, alone amid a waste of wild air and brackish waters
and the sea-harvest of shells and tangle and veiled grey sunlight
and gay-clad light-clad figures of children and girls and voices   5
childish and girlish in the air.

A girl stood before him in midstream, alone and still,
gazing out to sea. She seemed like one whom magic had
changed into the likeness of a strange and beautiful seabird.
Her long slender bare legs were delicate as a crane's and pure   10
save where an emerald trail of seaweed had fashioned itself as a
sign upon the flesh. Her thighs, fuller and soft-hued as ivory,
were bared almost to the hips, where the white fringes of her
drawers were like feathering of soft white down. Her slate-blue
skirts were kilted boldly about her waist and dovetailed behind   15
her. Her bosom was as a bird's, soft and slight, slight and soft
as the breast of some dark-plumaged dove. But her long fair hair
was girlish: and girlish, and touched with the wonder of mortal
beauty, her face.

She was alone and still, gazing out to sea; and when she felt   20
his presence and the worship of his eyes her eyes turned to him
in quiet sufferance of his gaze, without shame or wantonness.
Long, long she suffered his gaze and then quietly withdrew her
eyes from his and bent them towards the stream, gently stirring
the water with her foot hither and thither. The first faint noise   25
of gently moving water broke the silence, low and faint and
whispering, faint as the bells of sleep; hither and thither, hither
and thither; and a faint flame trembled on her cheek.

—Heavenly God! cried Stephen's soul, in an outburst of
profane joy.   30

He turned away from her suddenly and set off across the
strand. His cheeks were aflame; his body was aglow; his limbs
were trembling. On and on and on and on he strode, far out
over the sands, singing wildly to the sea, crying to greet the
advent of the life that had cried to him.   35

Her image had passed into his soul for ever and no word
had broken the holy silence of his ecstasy. Her eyes had called
him and his soul had leaped at the call. To live, to err, to fall,
to triumph, to recreate life out of life! A wild angel had
appeared to him, the angel of mortal youth and beauty, an   40
envoy from the fair courts of life; to throw open before him in

an instant of ecstasy the gates of all the ways of error and glory.
On and on and on and on!

JAMES JOYCE, *A Portrait of the Artist as a Young Man*

1   What effect is Joyce trying to produce in the first paragraph?
Analyse the rhythm and the diction of these sentences. Can the
repetitions be justified?

2   'She seemed like one whom magic had changed into the
likeness of a strange and beautiful seabird' (lines 8–9). In the
development of this paragraph, has Joyce succeeded in giving the
impression that a chance idea is substantiated as Stephen continues
to stare at the girl?

3   Consider the structure of lines 16–19. What rhythmic effect is
Joyce trying to produce here? Is it appropriate to the subject matter?

4   Suggest an interpretation of 'to recreate life out of life' (line 39).

5   worship (line 21), holy (line 37), angel (line 39), envoy from
the fair courts of life (line 41): is the passage as a whole strong
enough to bear the weight of these words?

6   '. . . to throw open before him in an instant of ecstasy the gates
of all the ways of error and glory' (lines 41–2). How has the awareness of a dichotomy in life been prepared for in the external scene
described in the first two paragraphs?

COMPARATIVE STUDY

1   In the light of both extracts, what is the symbolic significance
of the 'trembling bridge' which Stephen crosses?

2   Consider the importance of the sea and water in these passages.
How are they used to illuminate Stephen's experience?

3   Apart from the asceticism which Stephen appears to reject in
the first paragraph of *A*, two other elements of his life are conveyed
in these extracts. What are they?

4   Do the questions that Stephen asks himself in *A* (lines 40–7)
find an answer in *B*? Is it likely to be a final answer? Does the state

of mind revealed here throw any light on the making, and the nature, of a writer?

5   Consider the way in which the idea of holiness is modified throughout these extracts.

6   One of the qualities Stephen looks for in prose is *suppleness* A (line 46). Has Joyce's prose this quality? (Consider the interplay between intention and style in A, (lines 32–40) and B, (lines 20–35).

Suggestions for further Reading

Sir Philip Sidney *An Apologie for Poetrie* (ed. J. Churton Collins), Oxford University Press 1907

William Wordsworth Preface to the *Lyrical Ballads*, Methuen's English Classics

P. B. Shelley *A Defense of Poetry*, Nonesuch Press 1951

S. T. Coleridge *Biographia Literaria*, Everyman's Library

I. A. Richards *Practical Criticism*, Routledge 1929

T. S. Eliot *The Use of Poetry and the Use of Criticism*, Faber 1933

Herbert Read *Collected Essays in Literary Criticism*, Faber 1938

C. Day Lewis *The Poetic Image*, Cape 1947

Owen Barfield *Poetic Diction*, Faber 1952

George Whalley *Poetic Process*, Routledge 1953

Robin Skelton *The Poetic Pattern*, Routledge 1956

W. H. Auden *Making, Knowing and Judging*, University Inaugural Lecture, Oxford University Press 1956

T. R. Henn *The Apple and the Spectroscope*, Methuen 1966

F. W. Bateson *English Poetry: A critical introduction*, Longmans 1966

Acknowledgments

For permission to use copyright material in this book, the author and publishers wish to thank the following:

Harvard University Press and the Trustees of Amherst College for 'Safe in their Alabaster Chambers' from The Poems of Emily Dickinson, edited by Thomas H. Johnson, the Belknap Press of Harvard University Press, copyright 1951, 1955, by The President and Fellows of Harvard College; M. B. Yeats, Macmillan & Co Ltd and The Macmillan Company of Canada Ltd for an extract from 'The Secret Rose' and 'He Bids his Beloved be at Peace' from The Collected Poems of W. B. Yeats; Faber & Faber Ltd for 'His Excellency' from Collected Shorter Poems 1927–1957 by W. H. Auden; Faber & Faber Ltd for 'On the Move' from The Sense of Movement by Thom Gunn; Faber & Faber Ltd for 'Essential Beauty' from The Whitsun Weddings by Philip Larkin; Laurence Pollinger Ltd and the Estate of the late Mrs Frieda Lawrence for 'Cypresses' from The Complete Poems of D. H. Lawrence, and an extract from The White Peacock; Robert Graves for 'Sick Love', 'The Cool Web' and 'The Bards' from Collected Poems 1965; Rupert Hart-Davis Ltd for 'Cynddylan on a Tractor' from Song at the Year's Turning by R. S. Thomas; Holt, Rinehart & Winston Inc and Jonathan Cape Ltd for 'The Most of It' from The Complete Poems of Robert Frost, copyright 1942 by Robert Frost; Cambridge University Press for an extract from R. C. Trevelyan's translation of Sophocles's Oedipus at Colonus; George Allen & Unwin Ltd for an extract from Gilbert Murray's translation of Sophocles's Oedipus at Colonus; Faber & Faber Ltd and Harcourt, Brace & World Inc for an extract from Robert Fitzgerald's translation of Sophocles's Oedipus at Colonus; Faber & Faber Ltd for 'Love Poem II' from Collected Poems by George Barker; Faber & Faber Ltd for two extracts from 'Ash Wednesday' from Collected Poems 1909–1962 by T. S. Eliot; Edward Arnold (Publishers) Ltd for two extracts from A Passage to India by E. M. Forster; Leonard Woolf for an extract from To the Lighthouse by Virginia Woolf; The

Hogarth Press Ltd for an extract from *Cider with Rosie* by Laurie Lee;
Mrs James Thurber and Hamish Hamilton Ltd for an extract from
'The Night the Bed Fell' from *My Life and Hard Times* by James Thurber,
copyright © 1933, 1961 James Thurber, published by Harper &
Row, New York, originally printed in *The New Yorker*; William
Heinemann Ltd and Charles Scribner's Sons for an extract from *The
Forsyte Saga* by John Galsworthy; J. M. Dent & Sons Ltd and the
Trustees for the Joseph Conrad Estate for an extract from *The End of
the Tether* by Joseph Conrad; The Hogarth Press Ltd for an extract
from *A Bar of Shadow* by Laurens van der Post; William Heinemann
Ltd for an extract from *The Power and the Glory* by Graham Greene; The
Trustees of the Hardy Estate, Macmillan & Co Ltd and The Macmillan
Company of Canada Ltd for an extract from *The Return of the Native* by
Thomas Hardy; A. D. Peters & Co for an extract from *A Handful of Dust*
by Evelyn Waugh; Dame Ivy Compton-Burnett and Chapman &
Hall Ltd for an extract from *A Family and a Fortune* by Ivy Compton-
Burnett; Random House Inc and Curtis Brown Ltd for an extract
from *Sanctuary* by William Faulkner, copyright 1931 and renewed
1958 by William Faulkner; The Executors of the Mary Webb Estate
and Jonathan Cape Ltd for an extract from *Precious Bane* by Mary
Webb; Curtis Brown Ltd and Michael Joseph Ltd for an extract from
Herself Surprised by Joyce Cary; The executors of the James Joyce
Estate and Jonathan Cape Ltd for two extracts from *A Portrait of the
Artist as a Young Man* by James Joyce.